STREET SPEAK
ESSENTIAL AMERICAN SLANG & IDIOMS
STUDENT BOOK 1

DAVID BURKE

DAVID HARRINGTON

TOKYO

Book Design and Production: Caslon Books
Copy Editor: Robert Dilley
Front Cover Illustration: Ty Semaka
Inside Illustrations: Ty Semaka

Copyright © 1998 by David Burke and David Harrington
Published by Caslon Books • 12206 Hillslope Street • Studio City, CA 91604-3603 • USA • 1-707-546-8878 •
E-mail: CaslonBook@AOL.com

All rights reserved.

Reproduction or translation of any part of this work beyond that permitted by section 107 or 108 of the 1976 United States Copyright Act without the permission of the copyright owner is unlawful. Requests for permission or further information should be addressed to the Permissions Department, Caslon Books Inc.

This publication is designed to provide accurate and authoritative information in regard to the subject matter covered. It is sold with the understanding that the publisher is not engaged in rendering legal, accounting, or other professional services. If legal advice or other expert assistance is required, the services of a competent professional person should be sought.

The persons, entities and events in this book are fictitious. Any similarities with actual persons or entities, past and present, are purely coincidental.

Student book. . . ISBN 1-891888-09-9
Workbook . . . . ISBN 1-891888-10-2
Cassette . . . . . ISBN 1-891888-11-0
Teacher's book. . ISBN 1-891888-12-9

ISBN 1-891888-09-9

Printed in the United States of America
10 9 8 7 6 5 4 3 2 1

This book is dedicated to "Ma" Burke. We couldn't have done it without you!

ACKNOWLEDGMENTS

Our special thanks goes to Nini Hirschsohn for her enthusiasm, encouragement, and support in this new project. Her insight, viewpoints, and warmth were not only greatly appreciated, but indispensable.

We are forever grateful to Ty Semaka, a hardworking, gifted, and magical illustrator who brought life to these pages with his clever and hilarious cartoons. Ty, you're the man!

Our special thanks to Charles LeBeau, Chris Bartlett and David Maher for their suggestions and valuable advice in the production of this book.

We are fortunate for having found Robert Dilley, a brilliant copyeditor (as well as David Burke's oldest, yes oldest, friend from Jr. High School). No one can turn a phrase nor mark up a page with red pen like you!

Last but not least, a very special and heartfelt debt of gratitude goes to Hisako Tahara for making all of this possible.

TABLE OF CONTENTS

LESSON TITLE	WORDS PRESENTED
1 **AT THE PARTY** *(I'm having a blast!)* **PAGE 2**	**THIS LESSON CONTAINS 10 NEW SLANG WORDS & IDIOMS** blast (to be a) • no, way get a grip (to) • put someone on (to) get a load of something (to) • rug get on someone's case (to) • unable to stand someone (to be) hunk. • what's up with…
2 **AT THE MARKET** *(What a rip-off!)* **PAGE 14**	**THIS LESSON CONTAINS 10 NEW SLANG WORDS & IDIOMS** checker • ring up (to) die for (to) • rip-off from scratch (to make something) • rock-bottom make one's mouth water (to) • slash prices (to) pick up (to) • veggies
3 **AT THE MOVIES** *(Let's get the show on the road!)* **PAGE 26**	**THIS LESSON CONTAINS 10 NEW SLANG WORDS & IDIOMS** act one's way out of a paper bag (to be unable to) • plug something (to) blockbuster • sellout bomb • sleeper get the show on the road (to) • two thumbs up (to give something) line • write-up
4 **ON VACATION** *(Let's grab a cab and hit the town!)* **PAGE 38**	**THIS LESSON CONTAINS 12 NEW SLANG WORDS & IDIOMS** B and B • sightseeing (to go) booked solid (to be) • sleep in (to) grab a cab (to) • soak up some sun (to) hang out (to) • stay up till all hours of the night (to) hit the town (to) • take a dip (to) put up for the night (to) • take in a movie (to)
5 **AT THE AIRPORT** *(I'm taking the red-eye)* **PAGE 50**	**THIS LESSON CONTAINS 12 NEW SLANG WORDS & IDIOMS** barf bag • layover boonies (in the) • red-eye bumped (to get) • standby (to be on) carry-on • travel light (to) frequent flyer • wiped out (to be) jet lag • wired (to be)

A CLOSER LOOK AT "REAL SPEAK"	ACTIVITIES	

T+Y = CH · D+Y = J
let you = **let'cha** / **chu**
what you = **what'cha** / **chu**
did you = **did'ja** / **ju**
would you = **would'ja** / **ju**
	Practice Using "Real Speak"
	`LISTENING`
	A. Wha'did they say?
	`SPEAKING`
	B. Did'ja or Didn't 'chu?
		Practice The Vocabulary
		`LISTENING`
		C. Context Exercise
		`GROUP - SPEAKING`
		D. Never-Ending Sentence
		`PAIR WORK - SPEAKING`
		E. Is it "Yes" or is it "No"?

T = D
Wha**d** a beau**d**iful ci**d**y!
Look a**d** it!
Grea**d** idea!
	Practice Using "Real Speak"
	`SPEAKING`
	A. "T" Pronounced Like "D"
	`LISTENING`
	B. Right or Wrong
		Practice The Vocabulary
		`LISTENING`
		C. TV Commercial
		`PAIR WORK - SPEAKING`
		D. You Say, I Say

MUST HAVE = MUST 'A
The movie **must'a** been a sellout.
They **must'a** plugged the movie in Paris.
The play **must'a** gotten a good write-up.
	Practice Using "Real Speak"
	`LISTENING`
	A. Should'a, Could'a Would'a, Must'a
		Practice The Vocabulary
		`LISTENING`
		B. I Know the Answer, But What's the Question?
		`GROUP - SPEAKING`
		C. Find Your Perfect Match
		`SPEAKING`
		D. Imagine That...

AND = 'N
Karen **'n** Steve are coming to visit.
Would you like some salt **'n** pepper?
Is the movie in black **'n** white?
	Practice Using "Real Speak"
	`SPEAKING`
	A. Put the Pair Back Together
		Practice The Vocabulary
		`LISTENING`
		B. It Could Happen
		`PAIR WORK - SPEAKING`
		C. Match the Sentences

TO = TA or DA
How much will it cost **ta** ride the bus **ta** work?
I'd like **ta** take a trip **ta** Tokyo this summer.
We went **ta** Paris **ta** study this year.
	Practice Using "Real Speak"
	`LISTENING`
	A. "Across" Word Puzzle
	`SPEAKING`
	B. "Ta Be" or not "Ta Be"
		Practice The Vocabulary
		`LISTENING`
		C. What You See Is Not What You Hear!
		`GROUP - SPEAKING`
		D. Once Upon a Time...
		`SPEAKING`
		E. Create Your Own Sentence

LESSON TITLE	WORDS PRESENTED
6 **AT A RESTAURANT** *(Let's grab a bite!)* **PAGE 62**	**THIS LESSON CONTAINS 12 NEW SLANG WORDS & IDIOMS** chocaholic — leftovers cut down on something (to) — on someone (to be) doggie bag — pig out (to) Dutch (to go) — side of something (a) eyes that are bigger than one's stomach (to have) — skip something (to) grab a bite (to) — sweet tooth (to have a)
7 **ON THE ROAD** *(Let's go for a spin!)* **PAGE 76**	**THIS LESSON CONTAINS 14 NEW SLANG WORDS & IDIOMS** blowout — lead foot (to have a) bumper-to-bumper traffic — pot hole clunker — punch it (to) cop — run a/the light (to) fender-bender — rush hour hauled in (to get) — spin (to take a) hop in (to) — total a car (to)
8 **AT SCHOOL** *(I had to pull an all-nighter!)* **PAGE 90**	**THIS LESSON CONTAINS 14 NEW SLANG WORDS & IDIOMS** ace a test (to) — killer blow a test (to) — make-up / make-up test cram (to) — mid-term cut class (to) — pop quiz drop a class (to) — psych final — pull an all-nighter (to) flunk (to) — straight A's
9 **TO YOUR HEALTH** *(I'm feeling under the weather)* **PAGE 104**	**THIS LESSON CONTAINS 14 NEW SLANG WORDS & IDIOMS** antsy (to be) — raring to go (to be) blah (to feel) — run a fever (to) bored out of one's mind (to be) — run its course (to) bounce back (to) — sick as a dog (to be as) in the pink (to be) — stir crazy (to go) pass out (to) — take it easy (to) pull through (to) — under the weather (to feel)
10 **ON A DATE** *(He stood me up!)* **PAGE 118**	**THIS LESSON CONTAINS 15 NEW SLANG WORDS & IDIOMS** ask someone out (to) — nerd blind date — no strings attached break a date (to) — puppy love crush on someone (to have a) — show up (to) drop-dead gorgeous — stand someone up (to) dump someone (to) — tie the knot (to) lead someone on (to) — turn someone down (to) love at first sight

A CLOSER LOOK AT "REAL SPEAK"	ACTIVITIES
GOING TO = GONNA I'm **gonna** go shopping today. We're **gonna** eat dinner early. Tom is **gonna** arrive at noon.	**Practice Using "Real Speak"** **SPEAKING** A. Going to "Gonna" **LISTENING** B. Correct or Incorrect **Practice The Vocabulary** **LISTENING** C. Listen and Match **LISTENING** D. You Always Have The Last Word **PAIR WORK - SPEAKING** E. Formal to Informal **REVIEW: "The Good, The Bad, and The…"**
WANT TO = WANNA I **wanna** go for a spin. We don't **wanna** get a blowout. **WANTS TO = WANSTA** He **wantsta** leave before rush hour. She **wantsta** sell her old clunker.	**Practice Using "Real Speak"** **PAIR WORK - SPEAKING** A. Wanna or Wansta **Practice The Vocabulary** **LISTENING** B. Cloze Exercise **LISTENING** C. Usage Mistakes **PAIR WORK - SPEAKING** D. Blank Blank **REVIEW: "In Other Words…Synonyms!"**
THE DISAPPEARING "H" What did **'e** say about the party? Look at **'im** run! **THE DISAPPEARING "TH"** He noticed three of **'em** standing there. I don't like Cindy and Ron. I never talk to **'em**.	**Practice Using "Real Speak"** **LISTENING** A. Two Missing Words **Practice The Vocabulary** **LISTENING** B. To Tell the Truth **PAIR WORK - SPEAKING** C. Paraphrasing - What's Another Way to Say…? **REVIEW: "A Fun Time Was Had By All"**
YOU = YA Do **ya** have any money? How are **ya**? Is that **yer** sister? **Y'r** my best friend. Is that dog **yers**?	**Practice Using "Real Speak"** **LISTENING** A. Unscramble **Practice The Vocabulary** **LISTENING** B. The Fading Conversation **ROLE PLAY - SPEAKING** C. Lights! Camera! Action! **PAIR WORK - SPEAKING** D. Tic-Tac-Toe **REVIEW: "The Night Shift"**
HAVE TO = HAFTA We **hafta** break our date. I **hafta** go out with the biggest nerd tonight. I **hafta** go out on a blind date.	**Practice Using "Real Speak"** **GROUP - SPEAKING** A. You Write the Songs **Practice The Vocabulary** **LISTENING** B. What Would You Do If Someone Said…? **PAIR WORK - SPEAKING** C. Create Your Own Story **REVIEW: "Some Opposites Do Attract"**

LESSON 1
AT THE PARTY
"I'm having a blast!"

GETTING STARTED — This lesson contains **10** new slang words & idioms.

A. MATCH THE PICTURES
Use the pictures to help you guess the meaning of the new slang words and expressions in the exercise on the opposite page.

STUDENT BOOK (PRE-INTERMEDIATE)

STREET TALK: *ESSENTIAL AMERICAN SLANG & IDIOMS*

READ THE SENTENCES AND CHECK THE BOX NEXT TO THE WORD OR PHRASE THAT BEST DEFINES THE SLANG OR IDIOM IN RED.

1. Don't be so upset. **Get a grip**!
   "*Get a grip*" means: ☐ Leave me alone! ☐ Calm down!

2. What a great party! I'm having a **blast**!
   "*I'm having a blast*" means: ☐ I'm terribly bored! ☐ I'm having a great time!

3. Rob seems a little upset. **What's up with** him?
   "*What's up with him*" means: ☐ What's wrong with him? ☐ What's he wearing?

4. That's not his real hair. I think it's a **rug**.
   "*I think it's a rug*" means: ☐ I think it's a hairpiece. ☐ I think it's a shirt.

5. That story can't be true. You're **putting me on**.
   "*You're putting me on*" means: ☐ You're disagreeing with me. ☐ You're teasing me.

6. **Get a load of** that dress. Isn't it ugly?
   "*Get a load of that dress*" means: ☐ Look at that dress. ☐ Buy that dress.

7. David exercises a lot. He's a **hunk**.
   "*He's a hunk*" means: ☐ He's an idiot. ☐ He's a muscular man.

8. **No way**! You can't do that! You're not allowed to come through here!
   "*No way!*" means: ☐ Absolutely! ☐ Absolutely not!

9. Stop reprimanding me. **Get off my case**!
   "*Get off my case*" means: ☐ Go on a trip! ☐ Stop criticizing me!

10. I'm not inviting Diane. I **can't stand** her.
    "*I can't stand her*" means: ☐ I really like her. ☐ I don't like her.

STUDENT BOOK (PRE-INTERMEDIATE)

AT THE PARTY • *"I'm having a blast!"*

DIALOGUE USING SLANG & IDIOMS

READ THE FOLLOWING DIALOGUE. CAN YOU UNDERSTAND ALL THE WORDS AND EXPRESSIONS IN RED?

Debbie and Becky are attending a party.

Debbie: I don't know why I let you convince me to come here. I hate parties.

Becky: Would you **get a grip**? This is going to be a **blast**!

Debbie: Oh, no. Look who just walked in. Sheila Hampton. I **can't stand** her. She always **got on my case** because she didn't like the way I dressed.

Becky: What?! Did you **get a load of** that tiny dress she's wearing? Her belt's so tight it looks like she's being cut in half! Hey, isn't that Ernie Milton she's with?

Debbie: Yeah, you're right. He's gained so much weight! And **what's up with** his hair?

Becky: What hair? I don't know what you think, but I think it's a **rug**.

Debbie: **No way**! You're **putting me on**! He was such a **hunk**! He's changed so much in ten years!

Becky: I remember. I wonder what happened to him. Uh oh. I think Sheila's waving at us. They're both coming this way!

Debbie: Oh, no. Run!

STREET TALK: *ESSENTIAL AMERICAN SLANG & IDIOMS*

DIALOGUE USING STANDARD ENGLISH

FILL IN THE BLANKS WITH THE CORRECT MEANING OF THE SLANG WORDS AND IDIOMS IN RED FROM THE OPPOSITE PAGE.

Debbie and Becky are attending a party.

Debbie: I don't know why I let you convince me to come here. I hate parties.

Becky: Would you _____? This is going to be a _____!

Debbie: Oh, no. Look who just walked in. Sheila Hampton. I _____ her. She always _____ because she didn't like the way I dressed.

Becky: What?! Did you _____ that tiny dress she's wearing? Her belt's so tight it looks like she's being cut in half! Hey, isn't that Ernie Milton she's with?

Debbie: Yeah, you're right. He's gained so much weight! And _____ his hair?

Becky: What hair? I don't know what you think, but I think it's a _____.

Debbie: _____! You're _____! He was such a _____! He's changed so much in ten years!

Becky: I remember. I wonder what happened to him. Uh oh. I think Sheila's waving at us. They're both coming this way!

Debbie: Oh, no. Run!

STUDENT BOOK (PRE-INTERMEDIATE)

AT THE PARTY • *"I'm having a blast!"*

THE SAME DIALOGUE USING "REAL SPEAK"

Debbie 'n Becky'er attending a pardy.

Debbie: I dunno why I letchu convince me da come here. I hate pardies.

Becky: Would'ju **ged a grip**? This'ez gonna be a **blast**!

Debbie: Oh, no. Look 'oo jus' walked in. Sheila Hampton. I **can't stand** 'er. She always **god on my case** 'cuz she didn' like the way I dressed.

Becky: What?! Didju **ged a load of** that tiny dress she's wearing? Her belt's so tide it looks like she's being cud 'n half! Hey, isn't that Ernie Milton she's with?

Debbie: Yeah, y'r right. He's gained so much weight! And **what's up with** 'is hair?

Becky: What hair? I dunno whatchu think, but I think it's a **rug**.

Debbie: **No way**! Y'r **pudding me on**! He was such a **hunk**! He's changed so much 'n ten years!

Becky: I remember. I wonder what happened ta him. Uh oh. I think Sheila's waving ad us. They're both coming this way!

Debbie: Oh, no. Run!

A CLOSER LOOK AT "REAL SPEAK"

t + y = ch

let you = *let 'chà / 'chu*
what you = *what 'cha / 'chu*

RULE: When a word ending in "t" is followed by a word beginning with "y," the "y" takes the sound of "ch."

d + y = j

did you = *did 'ja / 'ju*
would you = *would 'ja / 'ju*

RULE: When a word ending in "d" is followed by a word beginning with "y," the "y" takes the sound of "j."

HOW DOES IT WORK?

Did you eat yet?
↓
Did ✗ou eat ✗et?
↓
Did jou eat chet?
↓
Did juh eat chet?
↓
*Did'**ja** eat'**ch**et?*

In this sentence, the "y" in "you" follows a "d" and takes the sound of "*j*." The "y" in "yet" follows a "t" and takes the sound of "*ch*."

All unstressed short vowels or vowel combinations (such as the *ou* in "*you*") are commonly pronounced *uh* (often seen in the dictionary as the symbol: ə).

STREET TALK: *ESSENTIAL AMERICAN SLANG & IDIOMS*

PRACTICE USING "REAL SPEAK"

LISTENING

A. WHA'DID THEY SAY?
Listen to the sentences in "real speak" and place a check mark next to the corresponding long form below.

1. ☐ a. What do you do?
   ☐ b. What did you do?
   ☐ c. What don't you do?

2. ☐ a. I want you to leave.
   ☐ b. I wanted you to leave.
   ☐ c. I want to chew a leaf.

3. ☐ a. Did you finish your homework?
         No, Chet.
   ☐ b. Didn't you finish your homework?
         Not yet.
   ☐ c. Did you finish your homework?
         Not yet.

4. ☐ a. Why don't you get your car fixed?
   ☐ b. Why didn't you get your car fixed?
   ☐ c. Why don't you get her car fixed?

5. ☐ a. Is that a cheery book?
   ☐ b. Is that your book?
   ☐ c. Is the chair broke?

6. ☐ a. Did you eat, Chet?
         No, did you?
   ☐ b. Did you eat yet?
         No, did you?
   ☐ c. Did you cheat, Chet?
         No, did you?

JU or JA?

EXAMPLE	NOTE
Did 'ja eat 'chet? *No. Did 'ju?*	Notice that in the second line, the *ou* in "you" is now pronounced **'ju** instead of **'ja**. Why? Because now it's stressed.

SPEAKING

B. DID 'JA OR DIDN'T 'CHU?
Practice using **'ja**, **'cha**, **'ju**, and **'chu**. One person reads the question/statement, while the other reads the answer/response using the rule above.

Question / Statement | Answer / Response

Question / Statement	Answer / Response		
Did **'ja** go?	No. Did **'JU** go?	OR	No. Did **'JU**?
I thought **'cha** left yesterday.	Really? I thought **'CHU** left yesterday!	OR	Really? I thought **'CHU** did!
Did **'ja** finish your homework?	Yeah. Did **'JU** finish your homework?	OR	Yeah. Did **'JU**?
Could **'ja** help Steve?	No, could **'JU** help him?	OR	No, could **'JU**?

STUDENT BOOK (PRE-INTERMEDIATE)

AT THE PARTY • *"I'm having a blast!"*

PRACTICE THE VOCABULARY

LISTENING

C. CONTEXT EXERCISE
Listen to the short conversations. Decide whether the slang used makes sense or doesn't make sense. Circle your answer.

MAKES SENSE   DOESN'T MAKE SENSE

MAKES SENSE   DOESN'T MAKE SENSE

MAKES SENSE   DOESN'T MAKE SENSE

MAKES SENSE   DOESN'T MAKE SENSE

MAKES SENSE   DOESN'T MAKE SENSE

MAKES SENSE   DOESN'T MAKE SENSE

MAKES SENSE   DOESN'T MAKE SENSE

MAKES SENSE   DOESN'T MAKE SENSE

MAKES SENSE   DOESN'T MAKE SENSE

STUDENT BOOK (PRE-INTERMEDIATE)

SPEAKING

D. NEVER-ENDING SENTENCE

The first person starts a sentence with *"I can't stand broccoli."* Go around the class having each person repeat what has already been said and then add a new word, creating a never-ending sentence.

- I can't stand broccoli.
- I can't stand broccoli or coffee.
- I can't stand broccoli or coffee or math.
- I can't stand broccoli or coffee or math or cats.
- I can't stand broccoli or coffee or math or cats or...

VARIATION: Now try it with --

I had a blast when I... • Get a load of that... • What's up with your... No way! I'd never... • My teacher got on my case because I... You're putting me on! I don't believe that... • Get a grip and stop worrying about...

NOTE: Positive sentences often use "and" between items. However, negative sentences usually use "or."
For example:

*Betty loves chocolate **and** pizza **and** amusement parks **and** parties **and**...*
*Eric has traveled to England **and** France **and** Germany **and** Italy **and**...*

*Frank doesn't like peanuts **or** raisins **or** big cities **or** dogs **or**...*
*Donna has never been to Australia **or** Canada **or** Russia **or** Spain **or**...*

STUDENT BOOK (PRE-INTERMEDIATE)

AT THE PARTY • *"I'm having a blast!"*

SPEAKING

PAIR WORK

E. IS IT "YES" OR IS IT "NO"? - *(Part 1)*
Person A: Ask Person B a "yes" or "no" question. Person B answers using a slang term or idiom from the word list below.
NOTE: One of the slang words or idioms will not be used!

	PERSON A		PERSON B
1.	Did you enjoy the party?	▶	Yes...
2.	Did you eat snails when you were in France?	▶	No...
3.	Are you telling me the truth?	▶	No...
4.	Don't you think Betty's hair looks strange?	▶	Yes...
5.	Do you think I'm acting too emotional?	▶	Yes...

WORD LIST
- ☐ get a grip
- ☐ had a blast
- ☐ what's up with
- ☐ can't stand
- ☐ no way
- ☐ putting you on

E. IS IT "YES" OR IS IT "NO"? - *(Part 2)*
Person B: Ask Person A a "yes" or "no" question. Person A answers using a slang term or idiom from the word list below.
NOTE: One of the slang words or idioms will not be used!

	PERSON B		PERSON A
6.	You and Susan are good friends, aren't you?	▶	No...
7.	Isn't Alan muscular?	▶	Yes...
8.	Do you see Karen over there in her expensive clothes?	▶	Yes...
9.	Does your mother criticize you a lot?	▶	Yes...
10.	Do you think that's Tony's real hair?	▶	No...

WORD LIST
- ☐ can't stand
- ☐ rug
- ☐ on my case
- ☐ putting you on
- ☐ hunk
- ☐ get a load of

STUDENT BOOK (PRE-INTERMEDIATE)

VOCABULARY - A Closer Look

blast (to be a) *exp.* to be a lot of fun, to be exciting.

example: Wasn't the party a **blast** last night? I've never had such a good time!

translation: Wasn't the party **a lot of fun** last night? I've never had such a good time!

as spoken: Wasn't the pardy a **blast** las' night? I never had such a good time!

VARIATION: **blast (to have a)** *exp.* to enjoy oneself greatly.

SYNONYM -1: **kick (to be a)** *exp.*

SYNONYM -2: **riot (to be a)** *exp.*

SYNONYM -3: **scream (to be a)** *exp.*

SYNONYM -4: **way cool (to be)** *exp.* (teen slang).

YOU DO IT: *It was a blast going to...*

get a grip (to) *exp.* to calm down.

example: I've never seen you so upset! If you don't **get a grip**, you're going to get an ulcer!

translation: I've never seen you so upset! If you don't **calm down**, you're going to get an ulcer!

as spoken: I've never seen you so upset! If ya don't **ged a grip**, y'r gonna ged 'n ulcer!

NOTE: The expression *to get a grip* refers to someone who is so upset that he/she needs to get a grip on his/her emotions.

VARIATION: **get a grip on oneself (to)** *exp.*

SYNONYM -1: **a hold of oneself (to get)** *exp.*

SYNONYM -2: **pull oneself together (to)** *exp.*

YOU DO IT: *Get a grip and stop...*

get a load of someone/something (to) *exp.* to look at someone/something, to observe.

example: **Get a load of** the new dress Irene is wearing! I've never seen anything like it!

translation: **Observe** the new dress Irene is wearing! I've never seen anything like it!

as spoken: **Ged a load 'a** the new dress Irene's wearing! I've never seen anything like it!

SYNONYM: **check out someone/something (to)** *exp.*

YOU DO IT: *Get a load of that...*

AT THE PARTY • *"I'm having a blast!"*

get on someone's case (to) *exp.* to criticize someone.

example: Every time my aunt comes to visit, she **gets on my case** about how dirty the house is...and I clean it every day!

translation: Every time my aunt comes to visit, she **criticizes** me about how dirty the house is...and I clean it every day!

as spoken: Ev'ry time my aunt comes ta visit, she **gets on my case** about how dirdy the house is...an' I clean id ev'ry day!

SYNONYM: get on someone about something (to) *exp.*

YOU DO IT: *My friends get on my case when I...*

hunk *n.* a handsome and muscular man.

example: David used to be very thin and weak. Now he's become a **hunk**!

translation: David used to be very thin and weak. Now he's become a **handsome and muscular man**!

as spoken: David usta be very thin 'n weak. Now 'e's become a **hunk**!

SYNONYM: stud *n.*

YOU DO IT: *...is a real hunk!*

No way! *interj.* Absolutely not!

example: **No way!** I'm not going to let you do that because it's too dangerous.

translation: **Absolutely not**! I'm not going to let you do that because it's too dangerous.

as spoken: **No way!** I'm not gonna let chu do that 'cuz it's too dangerous.

SYNONYM: "Get real!" *interj.*

YOU DO IT: *No way! I'd never...*

put someone on (to) *exp.* to tease or kid someone.

example: I think Joe was **putting you on** when he said he was married. He just wanted to see your reaction.

translation: I think Joe was **kidding you** when he said he was married. He just wanted to see your reaction.

as spoken: I think Joe w'z **pudding you on** when 'e said 'e was married. He jus' wan'ed ta see yer reaction.

SYNONYM: yank someone's chain (to) *exp.*

YOU DO IT: *Susan was putting me on when she said...*

rug *n. (humorous)* hairpiece.

example: My father is starting to lose his hair. In another two years, he'll probably have to get a **rug**.

translation: My father is starting to lose his hair. In another two years, he'll probably have to get a **hairpiece**.

as spoken: My father's starding ta lose 'is hair. In another two years, he'll prob'ly hafta ged a **rug**.

YOU DO IT: *Bob wears a rug because...*

unable to stand someone (to be) *exp.* to be unable to tolerate someone, to dislike.

example: I **can't stand** our new math teacher. He always gives us homework on the weekend.

translation: I **can't tolerate** our new math teacher. He always gives us homework on the weekend.

as spoken: I **can't stand** 'ar new math teacher. He always gives us homework on the weekend.

SYNONYM: **unable to stomach someone (to be)** *exp.*

YOU DO IT: *I can't stand Carl because...*

What's up with... *exp.* What's the problem with...

example: **What's up with** your sister? She looks really upset about something!

translation: **What's the problem with** your sister? She looks really upset about something!

as spoken: **What's up with** yer sister? She looks really upsed aboud something!

SYNONYM -1: What's with... *exp.*

SYNONYM -2: What's the deal with... *exp.*

YOU DO IT: *What's up with...?*

LESSON 2 — AT THE MARKET

"What a rip-off!"

GETTING STARTED

This lesson contains **10** new slang words & idioms.

A. MATCH THE PICTURES
Use the pictures to help you guess the meaning of the new slang words and expressions in the exercise on the opposite page.

STREET TALK: *ESSENTIAL AMERICAN SLANG & IDIOMS*

MATCH THE WORDS IN RED WITH THE DEFINITION IN THE RIGHT COLUMN. WRITE THE LETTER OF THE DEFINITION IN THE BOX.

1. Did you taste this blueberry pie? It's **to die for**!
2. Why did you pay so much for that TV? What **a rip-off**!
3. If you're ready, I can **ring up** your purchases.
4. This store has **rock bottom** prices.
5. The lines in this market are so long. They need more **checkers**.
6. The market is **slashing** its prices.
7. My mother always says I have to eat all of my **veggies**.
8. These pastries are **making my mouth water**.
9. My mother made a cake **from scratch**.
10. I need to **pick up** some milk at the market.

A. thievery
B. buy
C. fantastic
D. making me hungry
E. calculate the cost of
F. cashiers
G. very low
H. from a recipe
I. vegetables
J. reducing

STUDENT BOOK (PRE-INTERMEDIATE) 15

AT THE MARKET • "What a rip-off!"

DIALOGUE USING SLANG & IDIOMS

READ THE FOLLOWING DIALOGUE. CAN YOU UNDERSTAND ALL THE WORDS AND EXPRESSIONS IN RED?

Bill and Liz are shopping for dinner.

Bill: Chicken is only twenty-nine cents a pound. Talk about **rock-bottom** prices!

Liz: I know. They've been **slashing** their prices all week.

Bill: I have an idea. Let's **pick up** some chicken and **veggies** and make a big salad tonight. We could also buy a cake for dessert.

Liz: Great idea! Look at this pastry section. It's **to die for**! Just look at all these cakes! The smell of these pastries is **making my mouth water**.

Bill: Wait! Did you see the price of these cakes? They cost more than the chicken. What a **rip-off**! Let's just make one **from scratch**. It'll be a lot cheaper.

Liz: I think you're right, but let's hurry so we can get the **checker** to **ring up** our order. I'm starving!

DIALOGUE USING STANDARD ENGLISH

CROSS OUT THE WORDS OR PHRASES THAT DO NOT HAVE THE SAME MEANING AS THE SLANG TERMS OR IDIOMS FROM THE OPPOSITE PAGE.

Bill and Liz are shopping for dinner.

Bill: Chicken is only twenty-nine cents a pound. Talk about **(low) (high)** prices!

Liz: I know. They've been **(increasing) (reducing)** their prices all week.

Bill: I have an idea. Let's **(buy) (sell)** some chicken and **(vitamins) (vegetables)** and make a big salad tonight. We could also buy a cake for dessert.

Liz: Great idea! Look at this pastry section. It's **(fantastic) (horrible)**! Just look at all these cakes! The smell of these pastries is **(making me sick) (making me hungry)**.

Bill: Wait! Did you see the price of these cakes? They cost more than the chicken. What **(thievery) (great prices)**! Let's just make one using **(a package mix) (a recipe)**. It'll be a lot cheaper.

Liz: I think you're right, but let's hurry so we can get the **(manager) (cashier)** to **(deliver) (calculate the cost of)** our order. I'm starving!

AT THE MARKET • *"What a rip-off!"*

THE SAME DIALOGUE USING "REAL SPEAK"

Bill 'n Liz'er shopping fer dinner.

Bill: Chicken's only twen'y-nine cents a pound. Talk about **rock-boddom** prices!

Liz: I know. They've been **slashing** their prices all week.

Bill: I have 'n idea. Let's **pick up** s'm chicken 'n **veggies** 'n make a big salad tanight. We could also buy a cake fer dessert.

Liz: Grade idea! Look 'it this pastry section. It's **ta die for**! Jus' look id all these cakes! The smell 'a these pastries is **making my mouth wader**.

Bill: Wait! Didju see the price of these cakes? They cost more th'n the chicken. Whad a **rip-off**! Let's jus' make one **fr'm scratch**. Id'll be a lot cheaper.

Liz: I think y'r right, b't let's hurry so we c'n get the **checker** da **ring up** 'ar order. I'm starving!

A CLOSER LOOK AT "REAL SPEAK"

T = D

RULE: When a "t" is between two voiced vowels, whether in a single word (such as: c**i**t**y**) or within a phrase (such as: Wh**at a** bea**ut**iful c**i**t**y**!) the "t" is often pronounced "d."

EXAMPLES	NOTES
Look a**t** this pastry section. Ok, bu**t** let's hurry. We can ge**t** the checker to ring up our purchases.	In these sentences, "t" retains its sound. Why? Because in each case, there is a vowel on only one side of the "t."
Talk about rock-bo**dd**om prices. Grea**d** idea! Just look a**d** all these cakes.	In these sentences, "t" is pronounced as a "d" because in each case, there is a vowel on both sides of the "t."

18   STUDENT BOOK (PRE-INTERMEDIATE)

STREET TALK: ESSENTIAL AMERICAN SLANG & IDIOMS

PRACTICE USING "REAL SPEAK"

SPEAKING

A. "T" PRONOUNCED LIKE "D"
STEP 1: Cross out all of the "T's" that are pronounced like "D's."
STEP 2: Repeat the sentence in "real speak."

1. What a beautiful sweater! Did you get it when you went shopping last Saturday?
2. My parents ordered a bottle of champagne for their anniversary.
3. My laptop computer is battery-operated.
4. What a great car! Is it an automatic?
5. Let's go to the party later. Betty said there's going to be a lot of good food there.

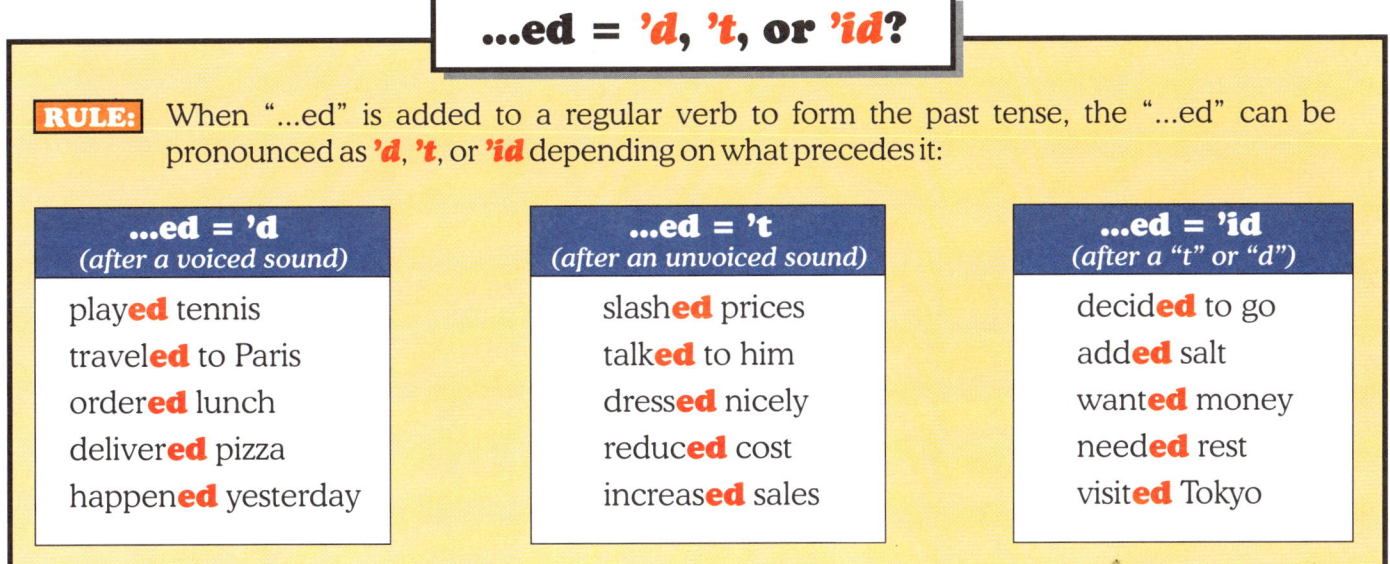

...ed = 'd, 't, or 'id?

RULE: When "...ed" is added to a regular verb to form the past tense, the "...ed" can be pronounced as 'd, 't, or 'id depending on what precedes it:

...ed = 'd (after a voiced sound)	...ed = 't (after an unvoiced sound)	...ed = 'id (after a "t" or "d")
played tennis	slashed prices	decided to go
traveled to Paris	talked to him	added salt
ordered lunch	dressed nicely	wanted money
delivered pizza	reduced cost	needed rest
happened yesterday	increased sales	visited Tokyo

LISTENING

B. RIGHT OR WRONG
Listen to the following sentences and decide if the pronunciation is right or wrong.

1. ☐ RIGHT ☐ WRONG
2. ☐ RIGHT ☐ WRONG
3. ☐ RIGHT ☐ WRONG
4. ☐ RIGHT ☐ WRONG
5. ☐ RIGHT ☐ WRONG
6. ☐ RIGHT ☐ WRONG

AT THE MARKET • *"What a rip-off!"*

PRACTICE THE VOCABULARY

LISTENING

C. TV COMMERCIAL
Listen to the commercial and answer the questions below.

Welcome to David's market!

QUESTIONS:

1. **At David's Market, what do they have in the produce department?**

   Answer: _____

2. **Who will ring up your purchases within five minutes?**

   Answer: _____

3. **What did the announcer suggest that you pick up from the bakery?**

   Answer: _____

4. **Are they raising or lowering prices at David's Market?**

   Answer: _____

5. **How are the chocolate cakes in the pastry department?**

   Answer: _____

6. **If you prefer to make the cake yourself, does the market have what you need?**

   Answer: _____

SPEAKING

D. YOU SAY, I SAY - (Part 1)

Person A goes first / Person B turns to the top of the next page.

Person A: Say the following sentences to Person B. Person B will give the appropriate response using the slang and idioms just learned.

For fun: If Person B's answer is correct, say *"You got it!"* which means "You're right!" in slang.
If Person B's answer is *not* correct, say *"You blew it!"* which means "You made a mistake" in slang.

1.	STATEMENT	Is that store very expensive?
	RESPONSE	**No, they have rock-bottom prices.**
2.	STATEMENT	I paid five hundred dollars for this sweater.
	RESPONSE	**What a rip-off!**
3.	STATEMENT	To stay so healthy, what do you eat?
	RESPONSE	**I eats lots of veggies.**
4.	STATEMENT	That's the most beautiful dress I've ever seen.
	RESPONSE	**I know! It's to die for!**
5.	STATEMENT	Why do your cakes always taste so good?
	RESPONSE	**I make them from scratch.**

D. YOU SAY, I SAY - (Part 2)

Person B will now read you some sentences. Answer with the appropriate response from the two choices given.

6.	STATEMENT	(Person B speaks)
	RESPONSE	Could you make it from scratch? Could you pick up some milk for me?
7.	STATEMENT	(Person B speaks)
	RESPONSE	It's making my mouth water. I eat lots of veggies.
8.	STATEMENT	(Person B speaks)
	RESPONSE	Because they're slashing their prices this week. Because it's a rip-off.
9.	STATEMENT	(Person B speaks)
	RESPONSE	No, it makes my mouth water. Yes, would you ring up my purchases?
10.	STATEMENT	(Person B speaks)
	RESPONSE	Yes, she eats lots of veggies. Yes, she's a checker.

AT THE MARKET • *"What a rip-off!"*

SPEAKING

D. YOU SAY, I SAY - *(Part 1)*
Person A will now read you some sentences. Answer with the appropriate response from the two choices given.

1.	STATEMENT	(Person A speaks)
	RESPONSE	No, they have rock-bottom prices. Yes, would you ring up my purchase?
2.	STATEMENT	(Person A speaks)
	RESPONSE	It's making my mouth water! What a rip-off!
3.	STATEMENT	(Person A speaks)
	RESPONSE	I eats lots of veggies. I know! It's to die for!
4.	STATEMENT	(Person A speaks)
	RESPONSE	I made it from scratch. I know! It's to die for!
5.	STATEMENT	(Person A speaks)
	RESPONSE	I make them from scratch. They have rock bottom prices.

D. YOU SAY, I SAY - *(Part 2)*
Person B, now it's your turn!

Person B: Say the following sentences to Person A. Person A will give the appropriate response using the slang and idioms just learned.

For fun: If Person A's answer is correct, say *"You got it!"* which means "You're right!" in slang.
If Person A's answer is *not* correct, say *"You blew it!"* which means "You made a mistake" in slang.

6.	STATEMENT	What would you like me to get for you from the market?
	RESPONSE	Could you pick up some milk for me?
7.	STATEMENT	That food smells wonderful.
	RESPONSE	It's making my mouth water.
8.	STATEMENT	Why do you want to go shopping at that store?
	RESPONSE	Because they're slashing their prices this week!
9.	STATEMENT	Are you finished with your shopping?
	RESPONSE	Yes, would you ring up my purchases?
10.	STATEMENT	Does your mother work at the supermarket?
	RESPONSE	Yes, she's a checker.

STREET TALK: *ESSENTIAL AMERICAN SLANG & IDIOMS*

VOCABULARY - A Closer Look

checker *n.* a cashier in a supermarket.

example: Look at the long line in this market! They need more **checkers**.

translation: Look at the long line in this market! They need more **cashiers**.

as spoken: Look 'it the long line 'n this market! They need more **checkers**.

NOTE: The *checker* works behind a *checkstand* where customers pay for their groceries.

YOU DO IT: *The checker at my grocery store always says...*

from scratch (to make something) *exp.* to make something from a recipe (using fresh ingredients as opposed to using instant mixes).

example: Your daughter made this cake **from scratch**? When I was her age, I was using package mixes!

translation: Your daughter made this cake **from a recipe**? When I was her age, I was using package mixes!

as spoken: Yer dauder made this cake **fr'm scratch**? When I w'z her age, I w'z using package mixes!

NOTE: **from square one (to make something)** *exp.* to make something by starting from the beginning.

YOU DO IT: *My mother makes ...from scratch.*

make one's mouth water (to) *exp.* said of something that increases one's appetite.

example: The smell of that fresh bread is **making my mouth water**!

translation: The smell of that fresh bread is **increasing my appetite**!

as spoken: The smell 'a that fresh bread's **making my mouth wader**!

YOU DO IT: *The smell of ...makes my mouth water!*

AT THE MARKET • *"What a rip-off!"*

pick up (to) *v.* to purchase, to buy.

example: I'm going to the market. Can I **pick up** something for you?

translation: I'm going to the market. Can I **purchase** something for you?

as spoken: I'm going ta the market. C'n I **pick up** something for ya?

SYNONYM: **grab (to)** *v.* (lit.): to take.

YOU DO IT: *The last thing I picked up at the store was...*

ring up (to) *v.* (said of a cashier) to calculate the cost of something.

example: I'm finally finished shopping! I'm going to find a cashier **to ring up** my groceries.

translation: I'm finally finished shopping! I'm going to find a cashier **to calculate the cost of** my groceries.

as spoken: I'm fin'lly finished shopping! I'm gonna find a cashier **da ring up** my groc'ries.

SYNONYM: **check out (to)** *v.* • **1.** to settle someone's account (at a market, hotel, etc.) **2.** to observe.

example (1): Sir, my checkstand is now open. I can **check you out** here if you'd like.

translation: Sir, my checkstand is now open. I can **settle your account** here if you'd like.

as spoken: Sir, my checkstand's now open. I c'n **check ya out** here if ya like.

example (2): **Check out** that beautiful new car!

translation: **Observe** that beautiful new car!

as spoken: **Check out** that beaudiful new car!

YOU DO IT: *Check out that...!*

rip-off *n.* (said of something overpriced) thievery, theft.

example: You paid a thousand dollars for that jacket? What a **rip-off**! I saw an identical jacket yesterday for a hundred dollars!

translation: You paid a thousand dollars for that jacket? What **thievery**! I saw an identical jacket yesterday for a hundred dollars!

as spoken: You paid a thousan' dollers fer that jacket? Whad a **rip-off**! I saw 'n idenical jacket yesterday fer a hundred dollers!

VARIATION: **rip** *n.* an shortened version of: *rip-off*.

ALSO: **rip someone off (to)** *exp.*

YOU DO IT: *Having to pay ...dollars for ... is a rip-off!*

STUDENT BOOK (PRE-INTERMEDIATE)

STREET TALK: ESSENTIAL AMERICAN SLANG & IDIOMS

rock-bottom *adj.* (said of a price) as low as possible, very inexpensive.

example: I'm going to buy a new car today. The dealer is selling them at **rock-bottom** prices!

translation: I'm going to buy a new car today. The dealer is selling them at **extremely low** prices!

as spoken: I'm gonna buy a new car taday. The dealer's selling 'em at **rock-boddom** prices!

YOU DO IT: *Our grocery store charges rock-bottom prices for...*

slash prices (to) *exp.* to reduce prices.

example: Do you want to go with me to the dress shop? They're **slashing their prices** today!

translation: Do you want to go with me to the dress shop? They're **reducing their prices** today!

as spoken: Wanna go with me da the dress shop? They're **slashing their prices** today!

SYNONYM: cut prices (to) *exp.*

YOU DO IT: *The new market is slashing their prices on...*

to die for *exp.* used to describe something that is wonderful (usually in reference to a food or thing).

example: I've never tasted such a wonderful pie in my life! It's **to die for**!

translation: I've never tasted such a wonderful pie in my life! It's **absolutely fantastic**!

as spoken: I've never tasted such a wonderful pie 'n my life! It's **ta die for**!

VARIATION: to die from *exp.*

YOU DO IT: *...is to die for!*

veggies *n.* a popular shortened version of "vegetables."

example: My mother made a great dinner last night. She served chicken, rice, **veggies**, and a wonderful dessert.

translation: My mother made a great dinner last night. She served chicken, rice, **vegetables**, and a wonderful dessert.

as spoken: My mother made a great dinner las' night. She served chicken, rice, **veggies**, an' a wonderful dessert.

YOU DO IT: *My favorite veggies are...*

STUDENT BOOK (PRE-INTERMEDIATE)

LESSON 3 — AT THE MOVIES

"Let's get the show on the road!"

GETTING STARTED

This lesson contains **10** new slang words & idioms.

A. MATCH THE PICTURES
Use the pictures to help you guess the meaning of the new slang words and expressions in the exercise on the opposite page.

26 STUDENT BOOK (PRE-INTERMEDIATE)

STREET TALK: *ESSENTIAL AMERICAN SLANG & IDIOMS*

DECIDE IF THE DEFINITION GIVEN FOR THE WORDS IN RED IS TRUE OR FALSE.

1. He **can't act his way out of a paper bag**.
   Definition: "is an excellent actor"
   ☐ True   ☐ False

2. I heard the movie is a **blockbuster**!
   Definition: "failure"
   ☐ True   ☐ False

3. The critic gave the movie **two thumbs up**.
   Definition: "a bad review"
   ☐ True   ☐ False

4. The movie was a total **bomb**.
   Definition: "success"
   ☐ True   ☐ False

5. Let's **get this show on the road**!
   Definition: "hurry and get started"
   ☐ True   ☐ False

6. The movie got a great **write-up**.
   Definition: "review"
   ☐ True   ☐ False

7. There are no tickets left. It's a **sellout**.
   Definition: "performance for which all of the tickets have been sold"
   ☐ True   ☐ False

8. They **plugged** the movie in Europe.
   Definition: "promoted"
   ☐ True   ☐ False

9. That unpopular movie turned out to be a **sleeper**!
   Definition: "successful movie"
   ☐ True   ☐ False

10. I have too many **lines** to memorize!
    Definition: "sentences"
    ☐ True   ☐ False

STUDENT BOOK (PRE-INTERMEDIATE)

AT THE MOVIES • *"Let's get the show on the road!"*

DIALOGUE USING SLANG & IDIOMS

READ THE FOLLOWING DIALOGUE. CAN YOU UNDERSTAND ALL THE WORDS AND EXPRESSIONS IN RED?

Kurt and David are at the movies.

Kurt: It's a good thing we got tickets early. The movie is a **sellout**!

David: They must have been **plugging** this movie for weeks. Now it's a **blockbuster**!

Kurt: The critics must be surprised that it turned out to be a **sleeper**.

David: I'll say. They said it was going to be a **bomb** and that the performers **couldn't act their way out of a paper bag.**

Kurt: Well, yesterday I saw a **write-up** where the reviewer gave it **two thumbs up**. He said there were a lot of funny **lines**.

David: Reviewers never seem to agree on anything. When is this thing going to start? It should have started an hour ago. Let's **get the show on the road**!

STREET TALK: ESSENTIAL AMERICAN SLANG & IDIOMS

DIALOGUE USING STANDARD ENGLISH

FILL IN THE BLANKS WITH THE CORRECT MEANING OF THE WORDS IN RED FROM THE OPPOSITE PAGE. CHOOSE FROM THE LIST BELOW.

Kurt and David are at the movies.

Kurt: It's a good thing we got tickets early. The movie is a _____!

David: They must have been _____ this movie for weeks. Now it's a _____!

Kurt: The critics must be surprised that it turned out to be a _____.

David: I'll say. They said it was going to be a _____ and that the performers _____.

Kurt: Well, yesterday I saw a _____ where the reviewer gave it _____. He said there were a lot of funny _____.

David: Reviewers never seem to agree on anything. When is this thing going to start? It should have started an hour ago. Let's _____!

sentences	a favorable critique
review	couldn't perform well
success after starting slowly	failure
promoting	big success
get started	performance that has sold all of its tickets

STUDENT BOOK (PRE-INTERMEDIATE)

AT THE MOVIES • *"Let's get the show on the road!"*

THE SAME DIALOGUE USING "REAL SPEAK"

Kurt 'n David 'er at the movies.

Kurt: It's a good thing we got tickets early. The movie's a **sellout**!

David: They must'a been **plugging** this movie fer weeks. Now it's a **blockbusder**!

Kurt: The cridics must really be saprised thad it turned out to be a **sleeper**.

David: A'll say. They said it w'z gonna be a **bomb** 'n th't the performers **couldn' act their way oud of a paper bag**.

Kurt: Well, yesderday I saw a **wride-up** where the reviewer gave it **two thumbs up**. He said there were a lod 'a funny **lines**.

David: Reviewers never seem da agree on anything. When's this thing gonna start? It should'a starded 'n hour ago. Let's **get the show on the road**!

A CLOSER LOOK AT "REAL SPEAK"

MUST HAVE = MUST 'A

RULE: Often when a letter has a weak sound, it may be dropped completely. For example, the letters "h" and "v" in the word "have" are not pronounced in the phrase "must have."

HOW DO WE GET FROM "MUST HAVE" TO "MUST 'A"?

The movie must have been a sellout.
↓
The movie must hav̶e̶ been a sellout. — The "e" in "have" is silent.
↓
The movie must hav been a sellout.
↓
The movie must h̶a̶v̶ been a sellout. — The "h" and "v" in "have" are dropped.
↓
The movie must uh been a sellout.
↓
The movie must 'a been a sellout.

All unstressed short vowels or vowel combinations (such as the remaining *a* in *"have"*) are commonly pronounced *uh* (often seen in the dictionary as the symbol: ə).

STUDENT BOOK (PRE-INTERMEDIATE)

STREET TALK: *ESSENTIAL AMERICAN SLANG & IDIOMS*

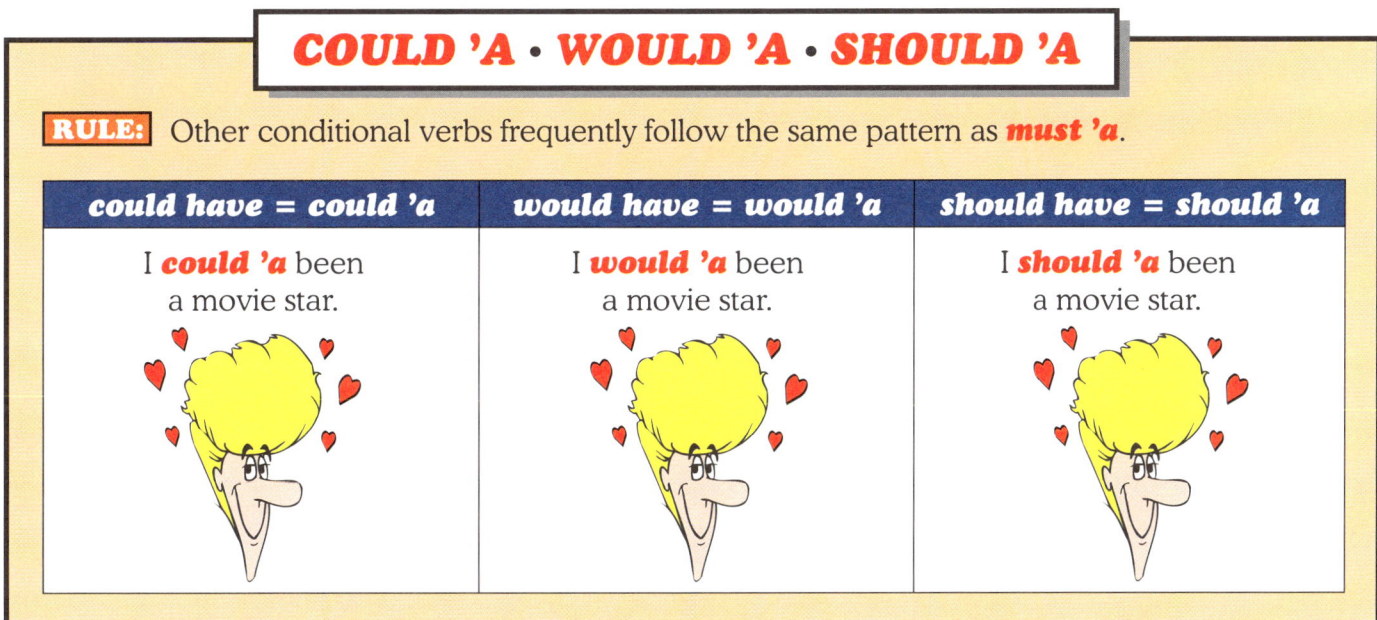

PRACTICE USING "REAL SPEAK"

LISTENING

A. SHOULD 'A, COULD 'A, WOULD 'A, MUST 'A
Listen to the following sentences which will be read naturally in "real speak." Write the words you hear in standard English using one letter for each space.

1. Hiromi didn't answer the phone. She _____ _____ been in the shower.
    ①   ②

2. You _____ _____ _____ there. The _____ was great!
      ①   ②   ③   ④

3. _____ __ all those packages. Lee _____ _____ _____ _____ for hours!
    ① ②   ③   ④   ⑤   ⑥

4. Tom Cruise _____ _____ _____ an academy award for his last movie.
                 ①   ②   ③

5. I _____ ' _____ _____ that movie ____ _____ __. It was horrible!
      ①   ②   ③   ④   ⑤   ⑥

6. __ _____ ___ _____ earlier, they _____ ____ ____ with us.
   ① ②   ③   ④   ⑤   ⑥   ⑦

7. You _____ ' _____ _____ such an expensive gift for my birthday.
          ①   ②   ③

8. Burt _____ _____ _____ lying or he _____ ' _____ _____ so nervous.
        ①   ②   ③   ④   ⑤   ⑥

STUDENT BOOK (PRE-INTERMEDIATE)   31

AT THE MOVIES • *"Let's get the show on the road!"*

PRACTICE THE VOCABULARY

LISTENING

LISTENING EXERCISE

B. I KNOW THE ANSWER, BUT WHAT'S THE QUESTION?
Listen to the answers and check the box next to the appropriate question.

1. *The answer is...*
Questions:
- ☐ Did Henry invite you to the opera?
- ☐ Did the critics enjoy the movie?
- ☐ Did your parents give you that book for your birthday?

2. *The answer is...*
Questions:
- ☐ Were you able to find the movie theater?
- ☐ Were you able to get tickets for the play?
- ☐ Were you able to make a reservation at the restaurant?

3. *The answer is...*
Questions:
- ☐ Do we have time to eat something before we leave?
- ☐ Would you like mustard on your sandwich?
- ☐ Do you listen to classical music?

4. *The answer is...*
Questions:
- ☐ Did you know that chicken is on sale at the market?
- ☐ Did you see the new car my parents just bought?
- ☐ Have you heard about the new bestselling book *Street Talk*?

5. *The answer is...*
Questions:
- ☐ Do you want to go see the new musical *Felines*?
- ☐ Did you play drums in the concert last night?
- ☐ Is your piano brand new?

6. *The answer is...*
Questions:
- ☐ That movie was a failure, wasn't it?
- ☐ That movie made a fortune, didn't it?
- ☐ That movie was very long, wasn't it?

7. *The answer is...*
Questions:
- ☐ Look at the long line! Didn't you say it wasn't popular?
- ☐ Look at the long line! Do you think they still have tickets left?
- ☐ Look at the long line! Do you mind waiting to buy a ticket?

STUDENT BOOK (PRE-INTERMEDIATE)

SPEAKING

SPEAKING EXERCISE

C. FIND YOUR PERFECT MATCH - *(Part 1)*
Answer the following questionnaire. Don't use the same answer twice.

1. The movie ( ) was a **blockbuster**.
2. I would give the movie ( ) **two thumbs up**.
3. I saw a good **write-up** for the movie ( ).
4. I think the movie ( ) will be a **sellout**.
5. The movie ( ) was a **sleeper**.
6. I think the actor ( ) **can't act his way out of a paper bag**.
7. I think ( ) was the best **line** I've ever heard in a movie.

What movie would you give two thumbs up?

I'd give the movie "The City" two thumbs up!

C. FIND YOUR PERFECT MATCH - *(Part 2)*
Next, go around the room and ask your classmates the following questions. Try to find someone who has the same answers as you. The person with the most matches wins.

1. What movie did you say was a blockbuster?
2. What movie would you give two thumbs up?
3. What movie did you see a good write-up for?
4. What movie do you think will be a sellout?
5. What movie did you say was a sleeper?
6. What actor do you think can't act his way out of a paper bag?
7. What line do you think was the best you've ever heard in a movie?

AT THE MOVIES • *"Let's get the show on the road!"*

SPEAKING

D. IMAGINE THAT...
Someone has presented you with a situation as seen below. Respond to each situation and make a complete sentence using one of the groups of words below. Use each group only once.

✓ blockbuster ✓ sleeper	✓ write-up ✓ sell-out	✓ two thumbs up ✓ lines
✓ plug ✓ blockbuster ✓ two thumbs up	✓ bomb ✓ act his way out of a paper bag	✓ sellout ✓ get the show on the road

IMAGINE THAT...
1. You've seen a great movie that you want to tell your friend about.

IMAGINE THAT...
2. Your friend asked you to describe the horrible TV show you saw.

IMAGINE THAT...
3. You are reviewing a fantastic new Broadway play.

IMAGINE THAT...
4. You want to convince your best friend to go with you to the ballet.

IMAGINE THAT...
5. Your friend wants to give you tickets to a concert. You don't like the group that's playing but your friend loves them. You want to refuse the tickets you don't want to hurt your friend's feelings.

IMAGINE THAT...
6. It's Saturday night and you are looking in the newspaper to find a good movie to go see with your family. You want to see a comedy but your brother wants to see an adventure movie. Explain why going to see the comedy would be better.

VOCABULARY - A Closer Look

act one's way out of a paper bag (to be unable to) *exp.* said of a bad actor.

- *example:* I saw a terrible movie on television last night. The actors **couldn't act their way out of a paper bag**!
- *translation:* I saw a terrible movie on television last night. The actors **were horrible**!
- *as spoken:* I saw a terr'ble movie on TV las' night. The acters **couldn' act their way oud of a paper bag**!
- **YOU DO IT:** ...**can't act his/her way out of a paper bag.**

blockbuster *n.* a very successful movie, play, film, etc.

- *example:* You have to go see the new play that just opened. It's a real **blockbuster**!
- *translation:* You have to go see the new play that just opened. It's a real **success**!
- *as spoken:* Ya hafta go see the new play th't just opened. It's a real **blockbuster**!
- **SYNONYM -1:** hit *n.*
- **SYNONYM -2:** smash *n.*
- **SYNONYM -3:** smash-hit *n.*
- **YOU DO IT:** **The movie ...was a blockbuster!**

bomb *n.* a complete failure (said of a movie, play, etc.).

- *example:* Poor Gina. She produced a movie with her own money and it turned out to be a **bomb**.
- *translation:* Poor Gina. She produced a movie with her own money and it turned out to be a **complete failure**.
- *as spoken:* Poor Gina. She praduced a movie with 'er own money 'n it turned out ta be a **bomb**.
- **SYNONYM:** dud *n.*
- **NOTE:** In the late nineties, teenagers created the expression *the bomb* meaning 'fantastic':
- *example:* That movie was **the bomb**!
- *translation:* That movie was **fantastic**!
- *as spoken:* That movie w'z **the bomb**!
- **YOU DO IT:** **The last ...I saw was a bomb.**

STUDENT BOOK (PRE-INTERMEDIATE)

AT THE MOVIES • *"Let's get the show on the road!"*

---

get the show on the road (to) *exp.* to start something, to begin.

example: Let's **get the show on the road**! The movie was supposed to start ten minutes ago.

translation: Let's **start the show**! The movie was supposed to start ten minutes ago.

as spoken: Let's **get the show on the road**! The movie w'z sapposta start ten minutes ago.

YOU DO IT: *Let's get the show on the road! We're late for...*

---

line *n.* a phrase or sentence that a performer memorizes from a script.

example: When I got hired to act in the movie, I thought it was going to be a very small part. But when I received the script, I discovered that I have pages and pages of **lines**!

translation: When I got hired to act in the movie, I thought it was going to be a very small part. But when I received the script, I discovered that I have pages and pages of **phrases to memorize**!

as spoken: When I got hired ta act in the movie, I thod it w'z gonna be a very small part. But when I received the script, I discovered th'd I have pages 'n pages of **lines**!

YOU DO IT: *...are the lines from (famous play or movie).*

---

plug something (to) *v.* to advertise or promote something.

example: When the actor was interviewed on television, he **plugged** his new movie.

translation: When the actor was interviewed on television, he **promoted** his new movie.

as spoken: When the acter w'z in(t)erviewed on TV, he **plugged** 'is new movie.

VARIATION: **give something a plug (to)** *exp.*

YOU DO IT: *I saw a commercial on TV plugging...*

---

sellout *n.* said of a performance for which all of the tickets have been sold.

example: I couldn't get tickets for the show at the Bijou tonight. It's a **sellout**!

translation: I couldn't get tickets for the show at the Bijou tonight. **All of the tickets have been sold**!

as spoken: I couldn't get tickets fer the show at the Bijou danight. It's a **sellout**!

YOU DO IT: *...was a sellout!*

STREET TALK: ESSENTIAL AMERICAN SLANG & IDIOMS

sleeper *n.* a success after starting slowly.

example: Megan's play was a bomb when it first opened, but it turned out to be a **sleeper**!

translation: Megan's play was a bomb when it first opened, but it turned out to be a **success after starting slowly**!

as spoken: Megan's play w'z a bomb when it first opened, bud it turned out ta be a **sleeper**!

YOU DO IT: *The movie ...was a sleeper.*

two thumbs up (to give something) *exp.* to critique something favorably.

example: Let's go see the movie around the corner. It should be really good. The critics **gave it two thumbs up**!

translation: Let's go see the movie around the corner. It should be really good. The critics **gave it a favorable review**!

as spoken: Let's go see the movie aroun' the corner. It should be really good. The cridics **gave it two thumbs up**!

NOTE: This expression comes from the popular television show featuring the two well-known critics, Siskel and Ebert, who each give a critique of a particular movie. At the end of both reviews, the home audience is shown either a fist with a thumb pointing up (for a favorable review) or a fist with a thumb pointing down (for an unfavorable review) below each critic's name. Many times the critics are not in agreement. However, when both give a favorable review, the audience is shown two thumbs up. This expression can be used in reference to only *one* person's favorable review: *I give the movie two thumbs up!*

YOU DO IT: *I would give the movie ...two thumbs up!*

write-up *n.* a written review of a play, show, etc.

example: Congratulations on your play! I read a great **write-up** about it in the Los Angeles Times!

translation: Congratulations on your play! I read a great **review** about it in the Los Angeles Times!

as spoken: C'ngradjalations on yer play! I read a great **wride-up** about it in the L.A. Times!

YOU DO IT: *I read a good/bad write up on...*

STUDENT BOOK (PRE-INTERMEDIATE)

LESSON 4 — ON VACATION

"Let's grab a cab and hit the town!"

GETTING STARTED — This lesson contains **12** new slang words & idioms.

A. MATCH THE PICTURES
Use the pictures to help you guess the meaning of the new slang words and expressions in the exercise on the opposite page.

STREET TALK: *ESSENTIAL AMERICAN SLANG & IDIOMS*

READ THE SENTENCES AND CHECK THE BOX NEXT TO THE WORD OR PHRASE THAT BEST DEFINES THE SLANG OR IDIOM IN RED.

1. Let's **take in a movie** tonight.
   - ❏ watch a movie
   - ❏ act in a movie

2. After working hard all week, it's nice to go to the beach and **hang out**.
   - ❏ play baseball
   - ❏ relax and do nothing

3. Instead of a hotel, let's stay in a **B and B**.
   - ❏ hotel with bed and breakfast
   - ❏ hotel with bath and beverage

4. Let's go to the pool and **take a dip**.
   - ❏ watch television
   - ❏ go swimming

5. You're so tan! Have you been **soaking up some sun** today?
   - ❏ staying inside
   - ❏ sunbathing

6. Let's **hit the town** and go shopping.
   - ❏ read a book
   - ❏ go into town

7. The hotel didn't have any rooms left. They were **booked solid**.
   - ❏ not yet cleaned
   - ❏ completely filled

8. I hope we can find a hotel **to put us up** for the night.
   - ❏ to lend us money
   - ❏ to accommodate us

9. In New York, you can either take the subway or **grab a cab** anywhere.
   - ❏ jump in front of a taxicab
   - ❏ take a taxicab

10. I'm tired because last night I **stayed up till all hours of the night**.
    - ❏ went to bed early
    - ❏ stayed awake late

11. I went **sightseeing** today. What a beautiful city!
    - ❏ visiting some interesting places
    - ❏ exercising

12. I usually get up early, but tomorrow I'm **sleeping in**.
    - ❏ getting up extra early
    - ❏ sleeping late

STUDENT BOOK (PRE-INTERMEDIATE)

ON VACATION • *"Let's grab a cab and hit the town!"*

DIALOGUE USING SLANG & IDIOMS

READ THE FOLLOWING DIALOGUE. CAN YOU UNDERSTAND ALL THE WORDS AND EXPRESSIONS IN RED?

Chris and Marie are on vacation.

Chris: It's a good thing this **B&B** was able to **put us up** for the night. All the hotels in town were **booked solid**.

Marie: So, what should we do now? Hey, I have an idea. Tonight, let's **grab a cab** and **hit the town**. Maybe we can go **sightseeing** before dinner.

Chris: And since we're on vacation, we can **stay up till all hours of the night** and **sleep in** tomorrow.

Marie: Great! Then in the afternoon, we can **take a dip**, then **hang out** by the pool and **soak up some sun**.

Chris: And tomorrow night, we could **take in a movie**!

DIALOGUE USING STANDARD ENGLISH

CIRCLE THE WORDS OR PHRASES THAT HAVE THE SAME MEANING AS THE WORDS IN RED ON THE OPPOSITE PAGE.

Chris and Marie are on vacation.

Chris: It's a good thing this **(hotel offering bed and breakfast) (hotel offering bath and barbecue)** was able to **(feed us) (accommodate us)** for the night. All the hotels in town were **(completely empty) (completely filled)**.

Marie: So, what should we do now? Hey, I have an idea. Tonight, let's **(find a taxicab) (drive a taxicab)** and **(go into town) (leave town)**. Maybe we can go **(visit the interesting places) (shopping)** before dinner!

Chris: And since we're on vacation, we can **(eat late) (stay awake late)** and **(get up early) (sleep late in the morning)** tomorrow.

Marie: Great! Then in the afternoon, we can **(go swimming) (exercise)**, then **(dry our clothes) (relax and do nothing)** by the pool and **(sunbathe) (take baths)**.

Chris: And tomorrow night, we could **(act in a movie) (go see a movie)**!

ON VACATION • *"Let's grab a cab and hit the town!"*

THE SAME DIALOGUE USING "REAL SPEAK"

Chris 'n Marie 'er on vacation.

LISTENING

Chris: It's a good thing this **B 'n B** w'z able da **pud us up** fer the night. All the hotels 'n town were **booked solid**.

Marie: So, what shu'we do now? Hey, I have 'n idea. Tanight, let's **grab a cab** 'n **hit the town**. Maybe we c'n go **sightseeing** b'fore dinner.

Chris: An' since w'r on vacation, we c'n **stay up till all hours 'a the night** 'n **sleep in** tamorrow.

Marie: Great! Then in the afternoon, we c'n **take a dip**, then **hang out** by the pool 'n **soak up s'm sun**.

Chris: An' tamorrow night, we could **take in a movie**!

A CLOSER LOOK AT "REAL SPEAK"

AND = 'N

RULE: Often in everyday conversation, when the word *"and"* connects two words, it is pronounced **'n**.

STANDARD ENGLISH	"REAL SPEAK"
Karen **and** Steve are coming to visit.	Karen **'n** Steve are coming to visit.
Would you like some salt **and** pepper?	Would you like some salt **'n** pepper?
Is the movie in black **and** white?	Is the movie in black **'n** white?
Tom went **and** saw the new museum.	Tom went **'n** saw the new museum.
We laughed **and** laughed for hours!	We laughed **'n** laughed for hours!
At the zoo, I saw lions **and** tigers **and** bears.	At the zoo, I saw lions **'n** tigers **'n** bears.

STREET TALK: ESSENTIAL AMERICAN SLANG & IDIOMS

PRACTICE USING "REAL SPEAK"

SPEAKING EXERCISE

SPEAKING

A. PUT THE PAIRS BACK TOGETHER

Below are some common pairs of words that are often connected by "and." Find the missing piece on the right that completes the pair on the left. Make sure to pronounce **"and"** in *real speak* as **'n**.

1. king and queen
2. in and
3. up and
4. left and
5. knife and
6. salt and
7. bread and
8. good and
9. peanut butter and
10. mustard and
11. top and
12. hot and
13. night and
14. breakfast, lunch, and
15. father and
16. sister and
17. husband and
18. shoes and
19. eyes and
20. right and
21. bacon and
22. cats and

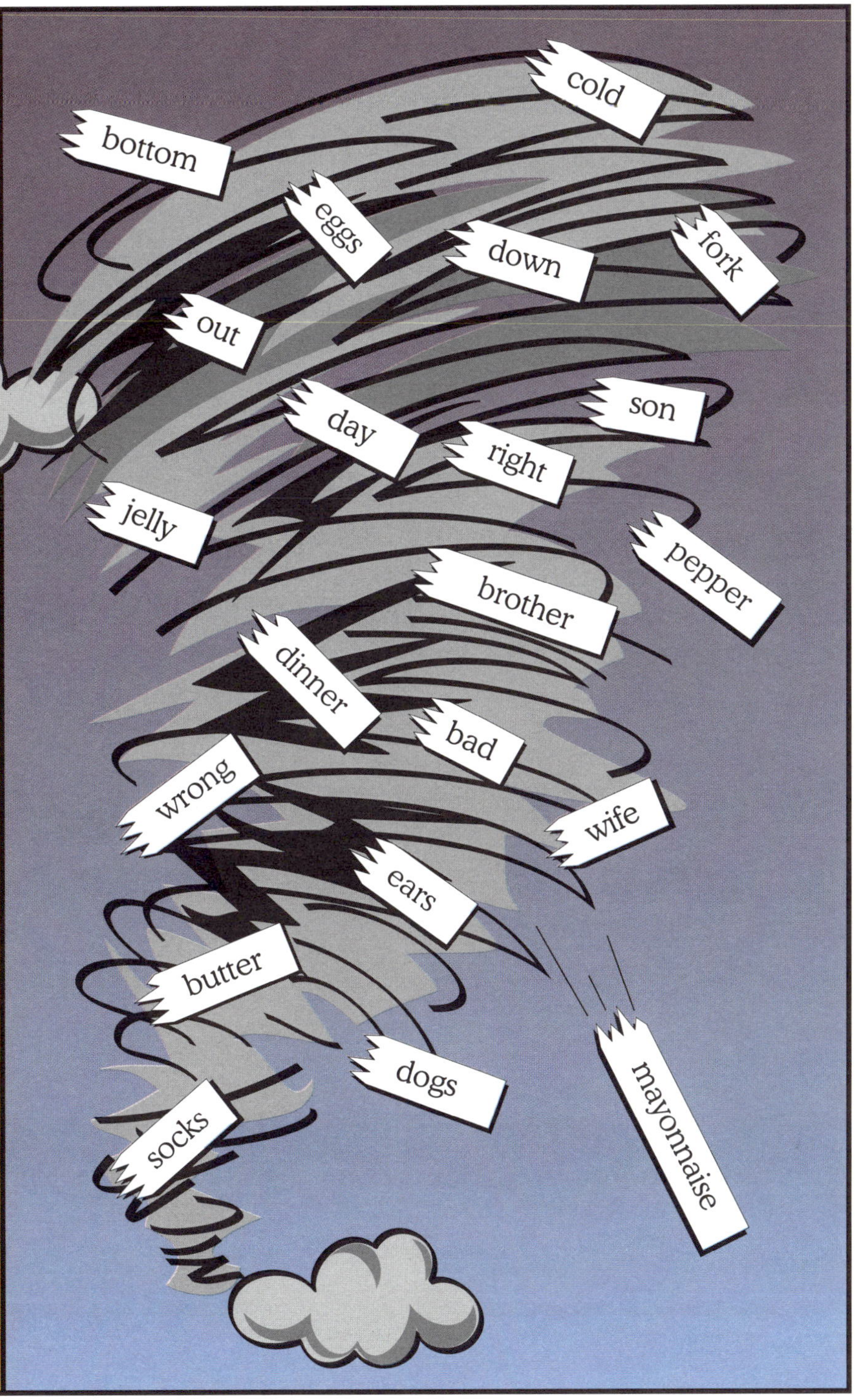

Word bank: cold, bottom, eggs, down, fork, out, son, day, right, pepper, jelly, brother, dinner, bad, wrong, wife, ears, butter, dogs, socks, mayonnaise

ON VACATION • *"Let's grab a cab and hit the town!"*

PRACTICE THE VOCABULARY

LISTENING

LISTENING EXERCISE

B. IT COULD HAPPEN
Listen to the questions and decide whether the situation is absolutely possible, not possible, or somewhere in between. Circle the slang answer below: *you betcha!* = absolutely possible • *it's almost sure fire* = somewhat possible • *iffy* = possible • *don't count on it* = doubtful • *no way!* = impossible.

1. YOU BETCHA! — IT'S ALMOST SURE FIRE — IFFY — DON'T COUNT ON IT — NO WAY!
2. YOU BETCHA! — IT'S ALMOST SURE FIRE — IFFY — DON'T COUNT ON IT — NO WAY!
3. YOU BETCHA! — IT'S ALMOST SURE FIRE — IFFY — DON'T COUNT ON IT — NO WAY!
4. YOU BETCHA! — IT'S ALMOST SURE FIRE — IFFY — DON'T COUNT ON IT — NO WAY!
5. YOU BETCHA! — IT'S ALMOST SURE FIRE — IFFY — DON'T COUNT ON IT — NO WAY!
6. YOU BETCHA! — IT'S ALMOST SURE FIRE — IFFY — DON'T COUNT ON IT — NO WAY!
7. YOU BETCHA! — IT'S ALMOST SURE FIRE — IFFY — DON'T COUNT ON IT — NO WAY!
8. YOU BETCHA! — IT'S ALMOST SURE FIRE — IFFY — DON'T COUNT ON IT — NO WAY!

STUDENT BOOK (PRE-INTERMEDIATE)

SPEAKING

C. MATCH THE SENTENCES - *(Part 1)*
Person A goes first · Person B turns to the next page.
Step 1: Call out a letter between A and L. Person B will call out a number between 1 and 12.
Step 2: Person B reads the sentence that corresponds to the letter that you called, and you read the sentence that corresponds to the number that Person B called.
Step 3: If the answers go together, write the letter and number in the answer box below.

PAIR WORK A

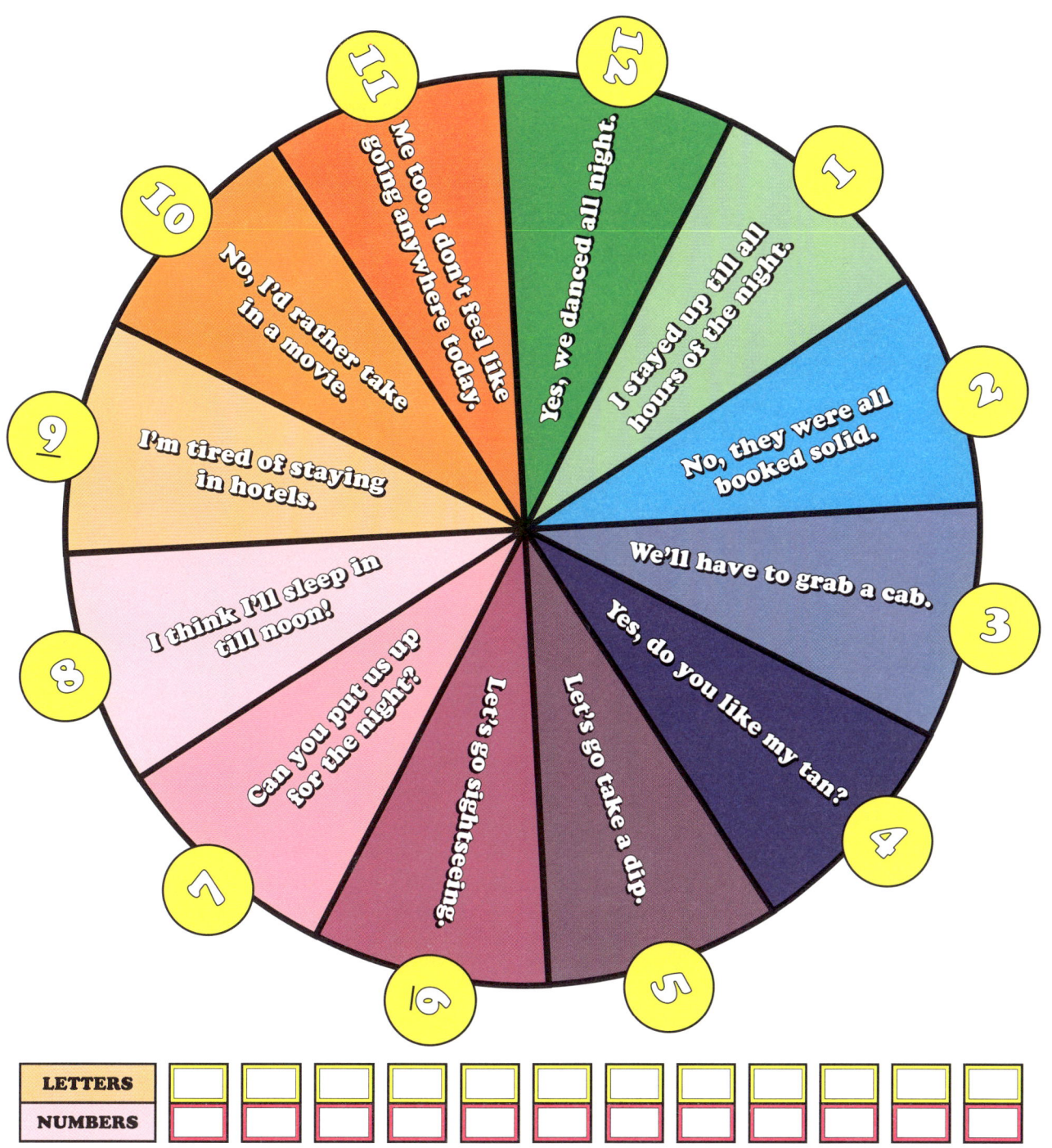

1. I stayed up till all hours of the night.
2. No, they were all booked solid.
3. We'll have to grab a cab.
4. Yes, do you like my tan?
5. Let's go take a dip.
6. Let's go sightseeing.
7. Can you put us up for the night?
8. I think I'll sleep in till noon!
9. I'm tired of staying in hotels.
10. No, I'd rather take in a movie.
11. Me too. I don't feel like going anywhere today.
12. Yes, we danced all night.

LETTERS											
NUMBERS											

ON VACATION • *"Let's grab a cab and hit the town!"*

SPEAKING

C. MATCH THE SENTENCES - *(Part 2)*

Step 1: Person A calls out a letter between A and L and you call out a number between 1 and 12.

Step 2: Read the sentence that corresponds to the letter that Person A called, and Person A reads the sentence that corresponds to the number that you called.

Step 3: If the answers go together, write the letter and number in the answer box below.

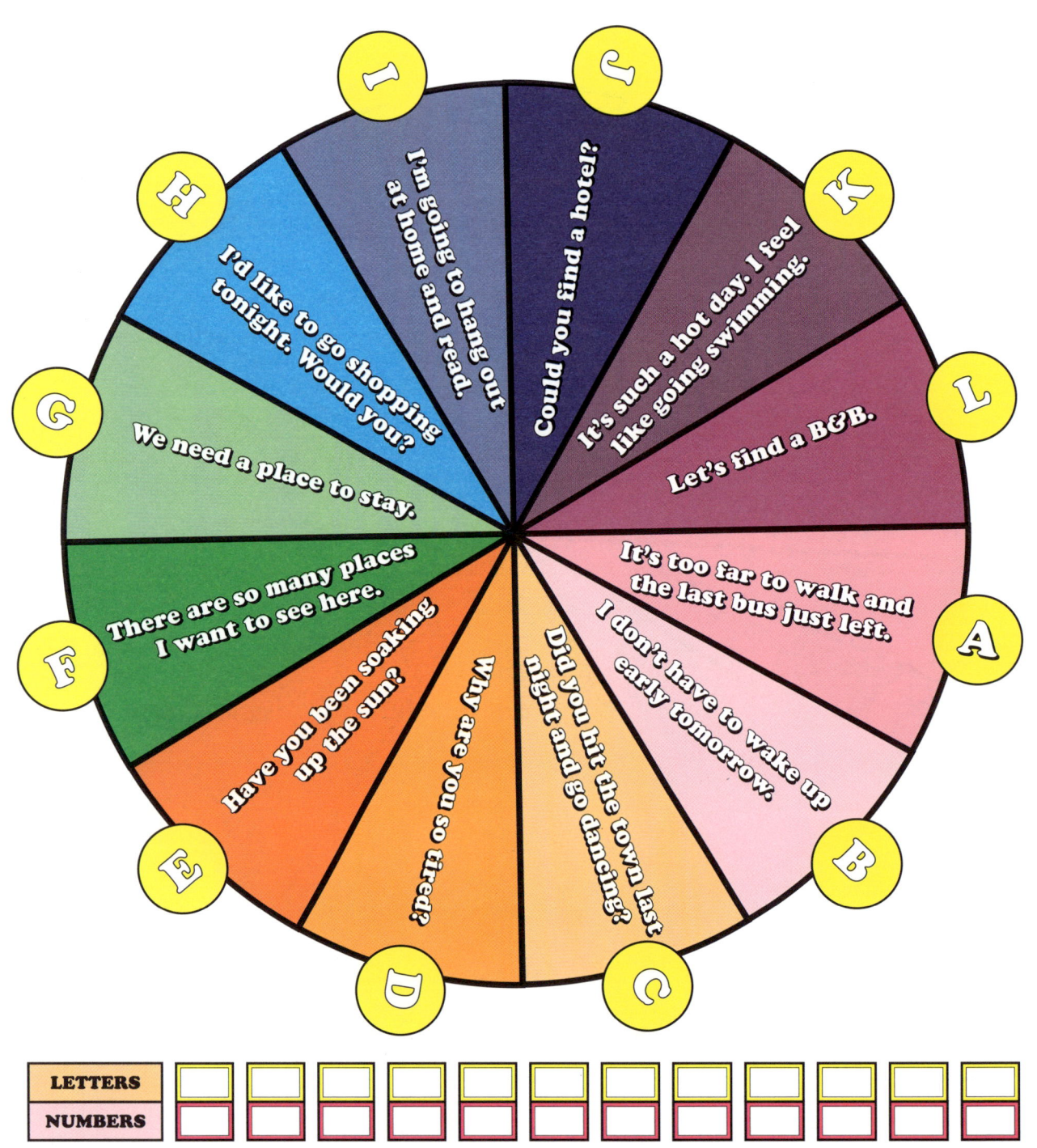

46 STUDENT BOOK (PRE-INTERMEDIATE)

STREET TALK: ESSENTIAL AMERICAN SLANG & IDIOMS

VOCABULARY - A Closer Look

B and B n. (an abbreviation for "bed and breakfast") generally a home converted into a hotel which offers guests a room for the night including breakfast.

- *example:* We stayed in a charming **B and B** in London last summer.
- *translation:* We stayed in a charming **bed and breakfast** in London last summer.
- *as spoken:* We stayed 'n a charming **B 'n B** 'n London las' summer.

YOU DO IT: *If I owned a B and B, I would name it...*

booked solid (to be) *exp.* to be completely full, to have no more space available (said of a hotel, cruise ship, airplane, etc. that requires a reservation).

- *example:* I wanted to stay at the famous Ritz Hotel in Paris, but it was **booked solid**.
- *translation:* I wanted to stay at the famous Ritz Hotel in Paris, but it was **completely full**.
- *as spoken:* I wan'ed ta stay 'it the famous Ritz Hotel 'n Paris, bud it w'z **booked solid**.

YOU DO IT: *I wanted to stay in a hotel in... but it was booked solid.*

grab a cab (to) *exp.* to take a taxi.

- *example:* Instead of trying to find parking, let's just **grab a cab** and go out to dinner.
- *translation:* Instead of trying to find parking, let's just **take a taxi** and go out to dinner.
- *as spoken:* Instead of trying da fin' parking, let's just **grab a cab** 'n go out ta dinner.

YOU DO IT: *It's best to grab a cab to go from .... to ...*

hang out (to) *exp.* to relax and do nothing.

- *example:* I'm going to **hang out** by the pool with Debbie today. Do you want to join us?
- *translation:* I'm going to **relax and do nothing** by the pool with Debbie today. Do you want to join us?
- *as spoken:* I'm gonna **hang out** by the pool with Debbie daday. Wanna join us?

YOU DO IT: *I usually hang out at...*

STUDENT BOOK (PRE-INTERMEDIATE)

ON VACATION • *"Let's grab a cab and hit the town!"*

hit the town (to) *exp.* to go into the main part of town where all the attractions are (usually for a night of fun, dining, dancing, movies, etc.).

    example: I'm bored tonight. I have an idea! Let's **hit the town** tonight and go out to dinner and a movie!

    translation: I'm bored tonight. I have an idea! Let's **go into the main part of town** tonight and go out to dinner and a movie!

    as spoken: I'm bored tanight. I have 'n idea! Let's **hit the town** tanight 'n go out ta dinner an' a movie!

    YOU DO IT: *I like to hit the town and...*

put up for the night (to) *exp.* to lodge for the night, to offer a place to stay for the night.

    example: We won't have to pay anything for a hotel when we go to Los Angeles. I have some friends there who can **put us up for the night**.

    translation: We won't have to pay anything for a hotel when we go to Los Angeles. I have some friends there who can **offer us a place to stay for the night**.

    as spoken: We won't hafta pay anything fer a hotel when we go da L.A. I have s'm frien's there who c'n **pud us up fer the night**.

    YOU DO IT: *When I go to ...'s house, he/she always puts me up for the night.*

sightseeing (to go) *exp.* to go look at the attractions and interesting sights.

    example: This is my first time in Rome. I can't wait **to go sightseeing**!

    translation: This is my first time in Rome. I can't wait **to go look at the attractions and interesting sights**!

    as spoken: This is my firs' time 'n Rome. I can't wait **ta go sightseeing**!

    VARIATION: **sightsee (to)** *v.*

    YOU DO IT: *I like going sightseeing in ...*

sleep in (to) *exp.* to sleep past the time one normally wakes up.

    example: Everyday, I wake up at six o'clock in the morning. But next week when I'm on vacation, I'm going to **sleep in**!

    translation: Everyday, I wake up at six o'clock in the morning. But next week when I'm on vacation, I'm going to **get up later than usual**!

    as spoken: Ev'ryday, I wake up 'it six a'clock 'n the morning. B't next week when I'm on vacation, I'm gonna **sleep in**!

    YOU DO IT: *I like to sleep in until...*

STREET TALK: ESSENTIAL AMERICAN SLANG & IDIOMS

soak up some sun (to) *exp.* to sunbathe.

example: I'm going to Hawaii tomorrow! I'm not going to do anything but **soak up some sun** and relax!

translation: I'm going to Hawaii tomorrow! I'm not going to do anything but **sunbathe** and relax!

as spoken: I'm going ta Hawaii damorrow! I'm not gonna do anything b't **soak up s'm sun** 'n relax!

SYNONYM: soak up some rays (to) *exp.*

YOU DO IT: *...is a great place to soak up some sun!*

stay up till all hours of the night (to) *exp.* to stay up all night long (having a good time, studying, watching television, etc.).

example: The party went on for hours! We **stayed up till all hours of the night** dancing!

translation: The party went on for hours! We **stayed up all night** dancing!

as spoken: The pardy wen' on fer hours! We **stayed up till all hours 'a the night** dancing!

YOU DO IT: *I stayed up till all hours of the night doing...*

take a dip (to) *exp.* to go swimming.

example: It's such a beautiful warm day today. I think I'll **take a dip**.

translation: It's such a beautiful warm day today. I think I'll **go swimming**.

as spoken: It's such a beaudif'l warm day daday. I think a'll **take a dip**.

SYNONYM: go for a swim (to) *exp.*

YOU DO IT: *Last summer I took a dip when I went to...*

take in a movie (to) *exp.* to go see a movie.

example: It's been raining all day long. Well, since we can't do anything outside, do you want to go **take in a movie**?

translation: It's been raining all day long. Well, since we can't do anything outside, do you want to go **see a movie**?

as spoken: It's been raining all day long. Well, since we can't do anything outside, wanna go **take in a movie**?

YOU DO IT: *The last time I took in a movie, I saw...*

STUDENT BOOK (PRE-INTERMEDIATE)

LESSON 5: AT THE AIRPORT

"I'm taking the red-eye"

GETTING STARTED

This lesson contains **12** new slang words & idioms.

A. MATCH THE PICTURES
Use the pictures to help you guess the meaning of the new slang words and expressions in the exercise on the opposite page.

STREET TALK: *ESSENTIAL AMERICAN SLANG & IDIOMS*

MATCH THE WORDS IN RED WITH THE BEST DEFINITION FROM THE RIGHT COLUMN. WRITE THE LETTER OF THE DEFINITION IN THE BOX.

1. ☐ I hate taking the **red-eye**. I always arrive so tired.
2. ☐ I don't take a lot of clothes with me when I go on business trips. I prefer to **travel light**.
3. ☐ Without a reservation, I was put on **standby**.
4. ☐ **I got bumped** because I was late.
5. ☐ I'm sorry I'm late. We had a three-hour **layover** in Texas.
6. ☐ As a **frequent flyer**, I was given a free ticket!
7. ☐ I got sick during the flight and needed a **barf bag**.
8. ☐ After not sleeping all night, I'm **wiped out**.
9. ☐ When I arrived in Paris, I was **wired**.
10. ☐ When you fly from LA to New York, do you get **jet lag**?
11. ☐ Lois lives in **the boonies**. I got lost five times!
12. ☐ I travel with only a **carry-on**.

A. delay (or wait)
B. tired from crossing time zones
C. a passenger waiting list
D. bag for vomiting
E. a distant and remote location
F. person who travels often
G. a small suitcase that can be carried on the plane
H. exhausted
I. late-night flight
J. had my airplane seat given away
K. take only a small suitcase
L. full of energy

STUDENT BOOK (PRE-INTERMEDIATE)

AT THE AIRPORT • *"I'm taking the red-eye!"*

DIALOGUE USING SLANG & IDIOMS

READ THE FOLLOWING DIALOGUE. CAN YOU UNDERSTAND ALL THE WORDS AND EXPRESSIONS IN RED?

Karen is at the airport waiting for Steve to arrive.

Steve: I'm sorry we're so late. We had an unexpected two-hour **layover** some place in **the boonies**. You know, I almost missed the flight entirely because of all the traffic! So I arrived late and **got bumped**. Luckily they agreed to put me on **standby**. All I had was a **carry-on** so it was easy.

Karen: It's a good thing you **travel light**. Well, with the **jet lag**, I imagine you're pretty **wiped out**.

Steve: Actually, I'm pretty **wired** after all that traveling. At least I got a free ticket for being a **frequent flyer**!

Karen: So, how was it traveling on the **red-eye**?

Steve: It got a little bumpy for a while. Luckily, I never had to use the **barf bag**!

STREET TALK: ESSENTIAL AMERICAN SLANG & IDIOMS

DIALOGUE USING STANDARD ENGLISH

FILL IN THE BLANKS WITH THE CORRECT MEANING OF THE WORDS IN RED FROM THE OPPOSITE PAGE. CHOOSE FROM THE LIST BELOW.

Karen is at the airport waiting for Steve to arrive.

Steve: I'm sorry we're so late. We had an unexpected two-hour _____ some place _____. You know, I almost missed the flight entirely because of all the traffic! So I arrived late and _____. Luckily they agreed to put me on _____. All I had was a _____ so it was easy.

Karen: It's a good thing you _____. Well, with the _____, I imagine you're pretty _____.

Steve: Actually, I'm pretty _____ after all that traveling. At least I got a free ticket for being a _____!

Karen: So, how was it traveling on the _____?

Steve: It got a little bumpy for a while. Luckily, I never had to use the _____!

airsickness bag	night flight	regular airline traveler
delay	a waiting list	travel with little luggage
exhausted	far away and remote	my seat in the airplane was given away
alert and energetic	time difference	small bag

STUDENT BOOK (PRE-INTERMEDIATE)   53

AT THE AIRPORT • *"I'm taking the red-eye!"*

THE SAME DIALOGUE USING "REAL SPEAK"

LISTENING

Karen's at the airport waiding fer Steve ta arrive.

Steve: I'm sorry w'r so late. We had 'n unexpected two-hour **layover** some place **'n the boonies**. Ya know, I almost missed the flide entirely 'cuz of all the traffic! So I arrived late 'n **got bumped**. Luckily they agreed da put me on **stan'by**. All I had w'z a **carry-on** so it w'z easy.

Karen: It's a good thing ya **travel light**. Well, with the **jet lag**, I imagine y'r preddy **wiped out**.

Steve: Acshelly, I'm preddy **wired** after all that trav'ling. At least I godda free ticket fer being a **frequent flyer**!

Karen: So, how w'z it trav'ling on the **red-eye**?

Steve: It god a liddle bumpy fer a while. Luckily, I never had da use the **barf bag**!

A CLOSER LOOK AT "REAL SPEAK"

TO = *TA* or *DA*

RULE: Often in everday conversation, "to" is pronounced "*ta*" following an unvoiced consonant. However, when following a voiced consonant or vowel, "to" is often pronounced "*da*."

TO = TA	TO = DA
How much will it cost **ta** ride the bus **ta** work?	I tried **da** learn French, but it was too hard.
I'd like **ta** take a trip **ta** Tokyo this summer.	Do you know the way **da** Hollywood from here?
He went **ta** Paris **ta** study this year.	Don't ask me **da** do that again!
We walked **ta** the park **ta** feed the pigeons.	Do you know how **da** fix the toaster?
We stopped **ta** have something **ta** eat.	She needs **ta** go **da** the dentist.

STUDENT BOOK (PRE-INTERMEDIATE)

STREET TALK: ESSENTIAL AMERICAN SLANG & IDIOMS

PRACTICE USING "REAL SPEAK"

LISTENING

A. "ACROSS" WORD PUZZLE
Listen to the sentences spoken in "real speak" and write the words you hear in standard English. Be sure to use one letter per space.

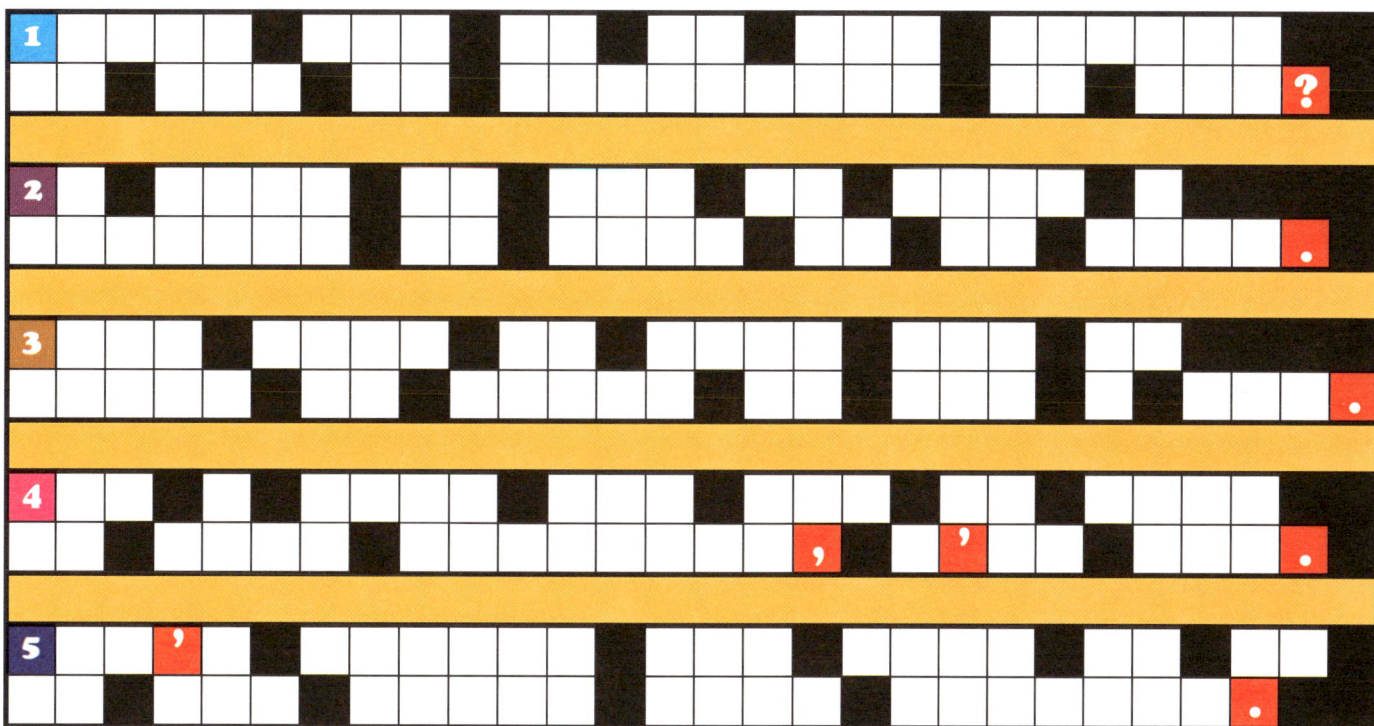

SPEAKING

B. "TA BE" OR NOT "TA BE..."
Say the following sentences in "real speak." *"ta"* and when to use *"da."*

1. I went **to** the market **to** pick up some bread.
2. Can you tell me how **to** get **to** the post office from here?
3. Steve wanted **to** go **to** the park but I wanted **to** go shopping instead.
4. I'd love **to** join you but I have work **to** do.
5. On the way **to** the airport, I had **to** stop **to** get gas.
6. We need **to** close the windows before it starts **to** rain.
7. I don't like **to** go **to** the dentist.
8. Jennifer's two friends were too tired **to** go **to** the movies.

STUDENT BOOK (PRE-INTERMEDIATE)   **55**

AT THE AIRPORT • *"I'm taking the red-eye!"*

PRACTICE THE VOCABULARY

LISTENING

C. WHAT YOU SEE IS NOT WHAT YOU HEAR!
Listen to the fairy tale. You'll notice that what you see on the page is not exactly what you hear. Circle the words that are different.

Once upon a time, there was a young girl named Cinderella who lived in the boonies and wanted something fun to do. So one day, she decided to use her frequent flyer miles and get a free ticket to somewhere exciting. She made an appointment to sell her script to a big producer in Hollywood. She always thought that her life story would make a good movie or even a musical!

Later that day, taking only a carry-on, she left for the airport. She always believed in traveling light. Unfortunately, when she arrived at the airport, she got bumped because she was late. So, she was put on standby for the next available flight. Finally, several hours later and completely wiped out, she was put on the red-eye for Hollywood, California!

The flight was so bumpy, that she started to feel airsick and feared that she might have to use the barf bag. Fortunately, just then the plane made a landing in Denver. After a two-hour layover, she was once again on her way to Hollywood, the land of fame and fortune.

By the time she arrived, she was so wired that she couldn't sleep and stayed up till all hours of the night. Unfortunately, the combination of no sleep and jet lag caused her to sleep in late and miss her appointment with the producer!

She was so disappointed that she decided to take the next flight back home. However, as fate would have it, she found herself sitting in the airplane next to Howard, a very handsome young man, formerly known as Prince.

Cinderella and Howard, formerly known as Prince, fell in love and moved to Chicago where they lived happily ever after in a double-wide mobile home.

STREET TALK: ESSENTIAL AMERICAN SLANG & IDIOMS

SPEAKING

D. ONCE UPON A TIME...
Make up a story beginning with "Once upon a time." Make sure to use one of the slang words from the list below. End your part of the story by selecting a different slang word for next person to use. Continue until all of the slang words have been used.

> Once upon a time, there was a fairy princess who took the **red-eye** to New York.

> Continue the story using **jet lag**...

> When she got there, she was very tired because she was suffering from **jet lag**.

> Continue the story using...

WORD LIST
- ☐ lay over
- ☐ barf bag
- ☐ wiped out
- ☐ frequent flyer
- ☐ standby
- ☐ bumped
- ☐ the boonies
- ☐ red-eye
- ☐ carry-on
- ☐ travel light
- ☐ jet lag
- ☐ wired

REVIEW — Now try using some slang words from previous chapters:
- ☐ blast
- ☐ hunk
- ☐ rip-off
- ☐ to die for
- ☐ sellout
- ☐ bomb
- ☐ sleep in
- ☐ hang out
- ☐ take a dip

STUDENT BOOK (PRE-INTERMEDIATE)

AT THE AIRPORT • *"I'm taking the red-eye!"*

SPEAKING

E. CREATE YOUR OWN SENTENCE

Choose a phrase from each column to create a sentence that makes sense. See how many original sentences you can make!

NOTE: To help you keep track of the sentences you've already used, write down the corresponding number under the appropriate column in the answer boxes at the bottom of the page.

COLUMN -A-	COLUMN -B-	COLUMN -C-
1. The tired woman	1. arrived late to the airport and	1. moved to Chicago.
2. The man	2. left his home in the boonies and	2. needed a barf bag.
3. Cousin Nancy	3. wanted to save money and	3. took the red-eye.
4. The movie star	4. had a layover in Boston and	4. was wiped out.
5. My boss	5. traveled for hours and	5. packed only one suit.
6. The flight attendant	6. received a free airplane ticket and	6. arrived late.
7. The frequent flyer	7. got so airsick and	7. got bumped.
8. Tyron, the famous artist,	8. traveled light and	8. went to Paris.

KEEP TRACK OF YOUR ANSWERS

COLUMN -A-	COLUMN -B-	COLUMN -C-	COLUMN -A-	COLUMN -B-	COLUMN -C-

STREET TALK: ESSENTIAL AMERICAN SLANG & IDIOMS

VOCABULARY - A Closer Look

barf bag *n.* a bag used for air sickness (usually in the back pocket of the seat in front of the passenger).

example: I sat next to a woman who was air sick during the entire flight. She never stopped using the **barf bag**.

translation: I sat next to a woman who was air sick during the entire flight. She never stopped using the **air sickness bag**.

as spoken: I sat next to a woman who w'z air sick during the entire flight. She never stopped using the **barf bag**.

YOU DO IT: *An unusual use for a barf bag is...*

boonies (in the) *n.* in a place that is far away and remote.

example: My grandmother lives **in the boonies**. It takes us hours to get to her house.

translation: My grandmother lives **in a far away and remote place**. It takes us hours to get to her house.

as spoken: My gran'ma lives **'n the boonies**. It takes us hours da get to 'er house.

SYNONYM: **boondocks (in the)** *n.*

YOU DO IT: *My friend ...lives in the boonies.*

bumped (to get) *v.* to have one's seat (in an airplane, train, etc.) given away to another passenger.

example: I **got bumped** for being five minutes late!

translation: I **had my seat given away to another passenger** for being five minutes late!

as spoken: I **got bumped** fer being five minutes late!

ALSO: **bumped up (to get)** *v.* to get upgraded to a higher class of travel.

YOU DO IT: *When I was traveling to ...I got bumped.*

carry-on *n.* a small bag which one can easily "carry on" and place in the airplane.

example: When you go to Paris for the week, just take a **carry-on**. That way you can avoid the long line at baggage claim.

translation: When you go to Paris for the week, just take a **small bag which you can easily carry with you on the airplane**. That way you can avoid the long line at baggage claim.

as spoken: When ya go da Paris fer the week, jus' take a **carry-on**. That way you c'n avoid the long line 'it baggage claim.

YOU DO IT: *In my carry-on, I always pack my...*

STUDENT BOOK (PRE-INTERMEDIATE)

AT THE AIRPORT • *"I'm taking the red-eye!"*

frequent flyer *n.* a person who travels by air often and is part of a special program offering free flights for those who travel frequently.

example: As a **frequent flyer**, once I've traveled 100,000 miles, I can get a free ticket to anywhere in the world!

translation: As a **member of the airline's special program offering free flights for those who travel often**, once I've traveled 100,000 miles, I can get a free ticket to anywhere in the world!

as spoken: As a **frequent flyer**, once I've traveled 100,000 miles, I c'n ged a free ticket ta anywhere 'n the world!

YOU DO IT: *As a frequent flyer, I got a free trip to...*

jet lag *n.* fatigue due to the time change between one's point of departure and one's destination.

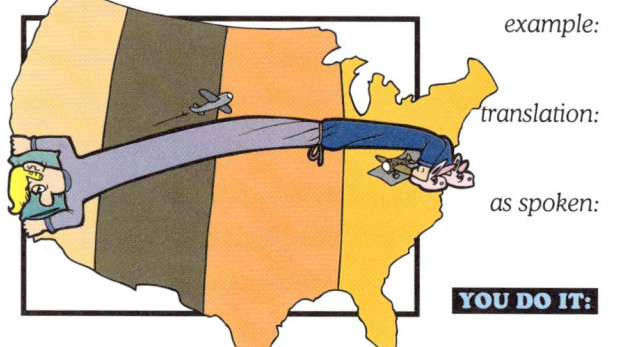

example: I never get **jet lag** when I travel to Europe. But when I travel back home, I'm exhausted!

translation: I never get **tired from the time change** when I travel to Europe. But when I travel back home, I'm exhausted!

as spoken: I never get **jet lag** when I travel da Europe. B't when I travel back home, I'm exhausted!

YOU DO IT: *The worst jet lag I had was when I traveled to...*

layover *n.* a delay in one or more cities when traveling by air.

example: On our way to Paris, we had a three-hour **layover** in Amsterdam.

translation: On our way to Paris, we had a three-hour **delay** in Amsterdam.

as spoken: On 'ar way da Paris, we had a three-hour **layover** 'n Amsterdam.

YOU DO IT: *The longest layover I ever had was...*

red-eye *n.* a long flight which occurs late at night and whose passengers arrive at their destination with "red eyes" from staying awake.

example: I'm taking the **red-eye** to New York instead of taking a flight during the daytime because I can save a lot of money.

translation: I'm taking the **late-night flight** to New York instead of taking a flight during the daytime because I can save a lot of money.

as spoken: I'm taking the **red-eye** ta New York instead of taking a flight during the daytime 'cuz I c'n save a lod 'a money.

YOU DO IT: *The last time I took a red-eye was...*

STREET TALK: *ESSENTIAL AMERICAN SLANG & IDIOMS*

standby (to be on) *n.* to be on a passenger waiting list for an available seat.

- *example:* Since I didn't have a reservation, the airline put me on **standby**.
- *translation:* Since I didn't have a reservation, the airline put me on **a passenger waiting list for an available seat**.
- *as spoken:* Since I didn't have a reservation, the airline put me on **stan'by**.

YOU DO IT: *I would fly standby if...*

travel light (to) *exp.* to travel with few pieces of luggage (usually only a small piece of luggage).

- *example:* I always **travel light**...even when I go overseas. Then I can buy lots of souvenirs!
- *translation:* I always **travel with a small light piece of luggage**...even when I go overseas. Then I can buy lots of souvenirs!
- *as spoken:* I always **travel light**...even when I go overseas. Then I c'n buy lots 'a souvenirs!

YOU DO IT: *When I travel light, I never pack my...*

wiped out (to be) *adj.* to be exhausted.

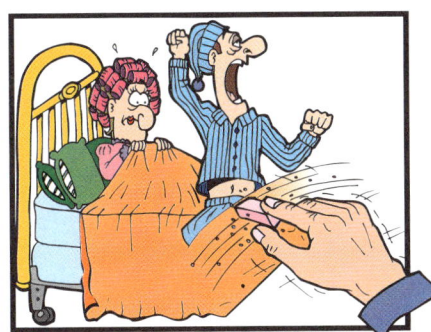

- *example:* After traveling for two days, I'm **wiped out**. All I want to do is go to bed!
- *translation:* After traveling for two days, I'm **exhausted**. All I want to do is go to bed!
- *as spoken:* After trav'ling fer two days, I'm **wiped out**. All I wanna do is go da bed!

YOU DO IT: *I'm wiped out because...*

wired (to be) *exp.* to be full of energy, excited.

- *example:* After all of this excitement today, I don't know how I'm going to sleep tonight. I'm so **wired**!
- *translation:* After all of this excitement today, I don't know how I'm going to sleep tonight. I'm so **energetic**!
- *as spoken:* After all 'a this excitement today, I dunno how I'm gonna sleep tanight. I'm so **wired**!

SYNONYM: **buzzed (to be)** *adj.* • **1.** to be extremely energetic • **2.** to be slightly intoxicated.

YOU DO IT: *I'm wired because...*

STUDENT BOOK (PRE-INTERMEDIATE)

LESSON 6 — AT A RESTAURANT

"Let's grab a bite!"

GETTING STARTED

This lesson contains **12** new slang words & idioms.

A. MATCH THE PICTURES
Use the pictures to help you guess the meaning of the new slang words and expressions in the exercise on the opposite page.

62   STUDENT BOOK (PRE-INTERMEDIATE)

STREET TALK: *ESSENTIAL AMERICAN SLANG & IDIOMS*

READ THE SENTENCES AND CHECK THE BOX NEXT TO THE WORD OR PHRASE THAT BEST DEFINES THE SLANG OR IDIOM IN RED.

1. I eat too much. I need to **cut down**.
   - ☐ eat less
   - ☐ eat more

2. Let's order hamburgers and **a side of** fries?
   - ☐ a small amount of
   - ☐ an additional order of

3. I'm going to **skip** the salad. I've eaten enough vegetables today.
   - ☐ omit
   - ☐ add

4. Let's **go Dutch** today and just split the bill.
   - ☐ pay separately
   - ☐ get someone else to pay

5. I love desserts. I have a **sweet tooth**.
   - ☐ dislike for sweets
   - ☐ strong desire for sweets

6. You're going to eat all that?! **Your eyes are bigger than your stomach**!
   - ☐ You always finish everything on your plate
   - ☐ You believe you can eat more than you can

7. I'll finish this sandwich tomorrow. I can eat the **leftovers** for lunch.
   - ☐ remaining food
   - ☐ freshly prepared food

8. Leave your money at home. Lunch **is on me**.
   - ☐ is going to be paid for by me
   - ☐ is going to be made by me

9. I'm hungry. Let's go **grab a bite**.
   - ☐ visit the dentist
   - ☐ eat something

10. I love chocolate! I'm a **chocaholic**.
    - ☐ chocolate hater
    - ☐ chocolate lover

11. What a meal! I really **pigged out**!
    - ☐ ate lightly
    - ☐ ate a lot

12. I'm full. I think I need a **doggie bag**.
    - ☐ bag to carry food home
    - ☐ bag of donuts

STUDENT BOOK (PRE-INTERMEDIATE)

AT THE RESTAURANT • *"Let's grab a bite!"*

DIALOGUE USING SLANG & IDIOMS

READ THE FOLLOWING DIALOGUE. CAN YOU UNDERSTAND ALL THE WORDS AND EXPRESSIONS IN RED?

Cecily and Jim are **grabbing a bite**.

Cecily: I know we were going to **go Dutch** for lunch, but since today is your birthday, lunch **is on me**.

Jim: Well, I was planning on **cutting down** but if you're paying, then I'm going to **pig out**!

Cecily: Good! It's your birthday! Have whatever you want. I feel like having a big juicy hamburger and **a side of** fries. How about you?

Jim: I'll have the same. I think I'll also get an order of onion rings, potato salad, baked beans, cole slaw, and some biscuits. And for my **sweet tooth**, I'll get a slice of chocolate pie. You know what a **chocaholic** I am!

Cecily: Jim, **your eyes are bigger than your stomach**.

Jim: Maybe you're right. Okay. **Skip** the salad.

Cecily: I have a feeling you're going to need a **doggie bag** for all the **leftovers**. And I'm going to need to get a second job to pay for this lunch!

STUDENT BOOK (PRE-INTERMEDIATE)

STREET TALK: *ESSENTIAL AMERICAN SLANG & IDIOMS*

DIALOGUE USING STANDARD ENGLISH

CIRCLE THE WORDS OR PHRASES THAT HAVE THE SAME MEANING AS THE WORDS IN RED ON THE OPPOSITE PAGE.

Cecily and Jim are **(getting something to eat) (leaving)**.

Cecily: I know we were going to **(go dancing) (pay separately)** for lunch, but since today is your birthday, **(I'll pay for) (you can pay for)** lunch.

Jim: Well, I was planning on **(leaving early) (dieting)** but if you're paying, then I'm going to **(talk a lot) (eat a lot)**!

Cecily: Good! It's your birthday! Have whatever you want. I feel like having a big juicy hamburger and **(an extra order of) (a small amount of)** fries. How about you?

Jim: I'll have the same. I think I'll also get an order of onion rings, potato salad, baked beans, cole slaw, and some biscuits. And for my **(wife) (desire for sweets)**, I'll get a slice of chocolate pie. You know what a **(chocolate lover) (chocolate hater)** I am!

Cecily: Jim, **(you have nice eyes) (you believe you can eat more than you can)**.

Jim: Maybe you're right. Okay. **(Take) (Eliminate)** the salad.

Cecily: I have a feeling you're going to need a **(bag used to carry food home) (purse)** for all the **(excess food) (tall people)**. And I'm going to need to get a second job to pay for this lunch!

STUDENT BOOK (PRE-INTERMEDIATE)

AT THE RESTAURANT • *"Let's grab a bite!"*

THE SAME DIALOGUE USING "REAL SPEAK"

Cecily 'n Jim'er **grabbing a bite**.

Cecily: I know we w'r gonna **go Dutch** fer lunch, b't since taday's yer birthday, lunch **is on me**.

Jim: Well, I w'z planning on **cudding down** b't if y'r paying, I'm gonna **pig out**!

Cecily: Good! It's yer birthday! Have whadever ya want. I feel like having a big juicy hamburger an' **a side 'a** fries. How 'bout chu?

Jim: A'll have the same. In fact, I think a'll also ged 'n order of onion rings, patado salad, s'm bake' beans, cole slaw, an' s'm biscuits. An' fer my **sweet tooth**, a'll ged a slice 'a choc'lit pie. Ya know whadda **choc'aholic** I am!

Cecily: Jim, **yer eyes 'er bigger th'n yer stomach**.

Jim: Maybe y'r right. Okay. **Skip** the salad.

Cecily: I have a feeling y'r gonna need a **doggie bag** fer all the **leftovers**. An' I'm gonna need da ged a secon' job da pay fer this lunch!

A CLOSER LOOK AT "REAL SPEAK"

GOING TO = GONNA

RULE: When "going to" is used to show future, it is often shortened (or *reduced*) to **gonna**.

HOW DO WE GET FROM "GOING TO" TO GONNA?

I'm *going to* pig out today.
⬇
I'm *goin͓ ͓o* pig out today.
⬇
I'm *goin o* pig out today.
⬇
I'm *goin o* pig out today.
⬇
I'm *guhn uh* pig out today.
⬇
I'm **gonna** pig out today.

In the phrase "going to," the hard sounds (or *full stop* sounds) of *g* & *t* disappear in everyday speech.

All unstressed short vowels or vowel combinations (such as the *oi* & *o* in *"going to"*) are commonly pronounced *uh* (often seen in the dictionary as the symbol: ə).

This shortened version of *"going to"* is so common that it has its own accepted spelling of: **gonna**.

STUDENT BOOK (PRE-INTERMEDIATE)

STREET TALK: ESSENTIAL AMERICAN SLANG & IDIOMS

PRACTICE USING "REAL SPEAK"

SPEAKING

A. GOING TO "GONNA"
Look at the sentences in the left column. Repeat the sentences in the right column replacing "going to" with "gonna."

1. I'm going to **pig out**.
2. I have a feeling you're going to need a **doggie bag**.
3. I'm going to start **cutting down** on desserts.
4. I'd like a hamburger but I'm going to **skip** the fries.

A. I'm _____ **pig out**.
B. I have a feeling you're _____ need a **doggie bag**.
C. I'm _____ start **cutting down** on desserts.
D. I'd like a hamburger but I'm _____ **skip** the fries.

GOING TO ≠ GONNA

RULE: "Going to" is never shortened to **gonna** when it indicates going from one place to another.

INCORRECT	CORRECT
Are you **gonna** the market?	Are you **going to** the market?
I'm **gonna** the movies tonight.	I'm **going to** the movies tonight.
Everyone was **gonna** the beach.	Everyone was **going to** the beach.

LISTENING

B. CORRECT OR INCORRECT
Listen to the sentences and decide if they are spoken correctly or incorrectly. Place an X in the appropriate box.

	1	2	3	4	5	6	7	8	9	10
CORRECT	☐	☐	☐	☐	☐	☐	☐	☐	☐	☐
INCORRECT	☐	☐	☐	☐	☐	☐	☐	☐	☐	☐

STUDENT BOOK (PRE-INTERMEDIATE)

AT THE RESTAURANT • *"Let's grab a bite!"*

PRACTICE THE VOCABULARY

LISTENING

C. LISTEN AND MATCH
Listen to the cassette and mark the appropriate illustration with a circle, triangle, diamond, square, or check mark.

 **CIRCLE**    **TRIANGLE**    **DIAMOND**    **SQUARE**    **CHECK**

LISTENING

D. YOU ALWAYS HAVE THE LAST WORD
Circle the sentence that best completes the conversation you hear.

1
Let's **grab a bite**.
I've got a **sweet tooth**.
I need a **doggie bag**.

2
Lunch is **on me**.
He's trying to **cut down**.
Let's **go Dutch**.

3
Did you **skip** lunch?
Do you have a **sweet tooth**?
Do you want **a side of** toast?

4
I'm not going to **pig out**.
There are no **leftovers**.
I'm not a **chocaholic**.

5
I'm trying to **cut down**.
Nancy has a **sweet tooth**.
I need a **doggie bag**.

6
Let's **grab a bite**.
I'm going to **pig out**.
I'd like **a side of** fries.

STUDENT BOOK (PRE-INTERMEDIATE)

SPEAKING

E. FORMAL TO INFORMAL - (Part 1)
Person A goes first / Person B turns to the top of the next page.

Person A: Say the following formal sentences to Person B who will repeat the sentence back to you using informal construction with one of the slang terms or idioms just learned.

For fun: If Person B's answer is correct, say *"You got it!"* which means "You're right!" in slang.
If Person B's answer is *not* correct, say *"You blew it!"* which means "You made a mistake" in slang.

1.	PERSON A	Would you like something to eat?
	PERSON B	**Do you wanna grab a bite?**
2.	PERSON A	Perhaps we should each pay our own portion of the bill.
	PERSON B	**Maybe we oughta go Dutch.**
3.	PERSON A	I will buy you lunch today.
	PERSON B	**Lunch is on me today.**
4.	PERSON A	I am trying to reduce my intake of desserts.
	PERSON B	**I'm trying to cut down on desserts.**
5.	PERSON A	I ate a lot of pizza last night.
	PERSON B	**I pigged out on pizza last night.**
6.	PERSON A	I would like to order French fries in addition to my hamburger.
	PERSON B	**I'd like a side of fries with my burger.**

E. FORMAL TO INFORMAL - (Part 2)
Person B will read you some formal sentences. Repeat the sentences using informal construction with one of the slang terms or idioms just learned.

7.	FORMAL	(Person B speaks)
	INFORMAL	**John's _____?**
8.	FORMAL	(Person B speaks)
	INFORMAL	**Nancy has _____.**
9.	FORMAL	(Person B speaks)
	INFORMAL	**My mom's a _____.**
10.	FORMAL	(Person B speaks)
	INFORMAL	**_____ the dessert. I'm on a diet.**
11.	FORMAL	(Person B speaks)
	INFORMAL	**I need _____.**
12.	FORMAL	(Person B speaks)
	INFORMAL	**There were _____.**

AT THE RESTAURANT • *"Let's grab a bite!"*

SPEAKING

E. FORMAL TO INFORMAL - *(Part 1)*
Person A will read you some formal sentences. Repeat the sentences using informal construction with one of the slang terms or idioms just learned.

PAIR WORK B

1.	FORMAL / INFORMAL	(Person A speaks) Do you wanna _____?
2.	FORMAL / INFORMAL	(Person A speaks) Maybe we oughta go _____.
3.	FORMAL / INFORMAL	(Person A speaks) Lunch is _____.
4.	FORMAL / INFORMAL	(Person A speaks) I'm trying _____.
5.	FORMAL / INFORMAL	(Person A speaks) I _____ last night.
6.	FORMAL / INFORMAL	(Person A speaks) I'd like _____.

E. FORMAL TO INFORMAL - *(Part 2)*
Person B, now it's your turn.

Person B: Say the following formal sentences to Person A who will repeat the sentence back to you using informal construction with one of the slang terms or idioms just learned.

For fun: If Person A's answer is correct, say *"You got it!"* which means "You're right!" in slang.
If Person A's answer is *not* correct, say *"You blew it!"* which means "You made a mistake" in slang.

7.	PERSON B / PERSON A	John believes his stomach capacity is greater than it is. **John's eyes are bigger than his stomach.**
8.	PERSON B / PERSON A	Nancy enjoys anything containing sugar. **Nancy has a sweet tooth.**
9.	PERSON B / PERSON A	My mother loves chocolate. **My mom's a chocaholic.**
10.	PERSON B / PERSON A	Omit the dessert. I'm on a diet. **Skip the dessert. I'm on a diet.**
11.	PERSON B / PERSON A	I need a container to take home this extra food from the restaurant. **I need a doggie bag.**
12.	PERSON B / PERSON A	There was a lot of uneaten food remaining from the party. **There were a lot of leftovers from the party.**

STUDENT BOOK (PRE-INTERMEDIATE)

STREET TALK: ESSENTIAL AMERICAN SLANG & IDIOMS

VOCABULARY - A Closer Look

chocaholic *n.* one who loves chocolate.

- *example:* My father is a **chocaholic**. He'll eat anything with chocolate on it!
- *translation:* My father is a **lover of chocolate**. He'll eat anything with chocolate on it!
- *as spoken:* My father's a **chocaholic**. He'll ead anything with choc'lit on it!
- **NOTE:** This is a play-on-words on the term *alcoholic*, meaning "a person addicted to alcohol." The suffix *-aholic* can be added to many words to suggest that the subject is addicted to something. For example: *food-aholic, shop-aholic, gym-aholic,* etc.
- **YOU DO IT:** *I think Kim is a chocaholic because...*

cut down on something (to) *v.* to eat less of something (usually in order to lose weight).

- *example:* I love desserts, but I'm trying **to cut down** because I've started to put on weight!
- *translation:* I love desserts, but I'm trying **to eat less of them** because I've started to put on weight!
- *as spoken:* I love desserts, bud I'm trying **ta cut down** 'cuz I've starded da pud on weight!
- **VARIATION:** **cut back on something (to)** *exp.*
- **ALSO:** **cut out something (to)** *exp.* to eliminate something completely from one's diet.
- **YOU DO IT:** *I'm trying to cut down on...*

doggie bag *n.* a bag used to carry leftover food home from a restaurant.

- *example:* I can't finish all this food. I'm going to ask our waiter for a **doggie bag**.
- *translation:* I can't finish all this food. I'm going to ask our waiter for a **bag to take this food home**.
- *as spoken:* I can't finish all this food. I'm gonna ask 'ar waider fer a **doggie bag**.
- **NOTE:** This term was originally used to refer to a bag that people could use to take bones home from a restaurant to their dog.
- **YOU DO IT:** *I need a doggie bag to take home this...*

STUDENT BOOK (PRE-INTERMEDIATE)

AT THE RESTAURANT • *"Let's grab a bite!"*

Dutch (to go) *exp.* to pay only for oneself.

example: Every time William and Steven eat at a restaurant, they **go Dutch**.

translation: Every time William and Steven eat at a restaurant, they **pay individually**.

as spoken: Ev'ry time William 'n Steven ead at a rest'rant, they **go Dutch**.

YOU DO IT: *David and I went Dutch to the...*

eyes that are bigger than one's stomach (to have) *exp.* to think one can eat more than one can.

example: You're going to eat all that food? I have a feeling **your eyes are bigger than your stomach**.

translation: You're going to eat all that food? I have a feeling **you think you can eat more than you can**.

as spoken: Y'r gonna ead all that food? I have a feeling **yer eyes 'er bigger th'n yer stomach**.

YOU DO IT: *My mom said my eyes are bigger than my stomach because...*

grab a bite (to) *exp.* to get something to eat.

example: I'm starting to get hungry. Do you want to go **grab a bite** somewhere?

translation: I'm starting to get hungry. Do you want to go **get something to eat** somewhere?

as spoken: I'm starding da get hungry. Wanna go **grab a bite** somewhere?

VARIATION: **grab a bite to eat (to)** *exp.*

YOU DO IT: *Yesterday I grabbed a bite at...*

leftovers *n.* remaining food that couldn't be finished.

example: Do you want to come to my house for dinner? We have a lot of **leftovers** from the party last night.

translation: Do you want to come to my house for dinner? We have a lot of **remaining food** from the party last night.

as spoken: Wanna come ta my house fer dinner? We have a lod 'a **leftovers** fr'm the pardy las' night.

YOU DO IT: *My favorite leftovers are...*

STREET TALK: ESSENTIAL AMERICAN SLANG & IDIOMS

on someone (to be) *exp.* to be treated to something by someone.

example: Since you did such a big favor for me yesterday, dinner **is on me**.

translation: Since you did such a big favor for me yesterday, **I'm paying for** dinner.

as spoken: Since ya did such a big faver fer me yesderday, dinner**'s on me**.

YOU DO IT: *In honor of your... lunch is on me.*

pig out (to) *exp.* to eat a lot, to eat like a pig.

example: I don't think I'm going to eat dinner tonight. I **pigged out** during lunch and I'm still full!

translation: I don't think I'm going to eat dinner tonight. I **ate a lot** during lunch and I'm still full!

as spoken: I don' think I'm gonna eat dinner tanight. I **pigged out** during lunch 'n I'm still full!

SYNONYM: pork out (to) *exp.*

YOU DO IT: *The last time I pigged out was...*

side of something (a) *n.* (used when ordering food) an extra order of something.

example: Since my hamburger doesn't come with anything extra, I'm going to get **a side of** cole slaw.

translation: Since my hamburger doesn't come with anything extra, I'm going to get **an extra order of** cole slaw.

as spoken: Since my burger doesn't come with anything extra, I'm gonna ged **a side 'a** cole slaw.

NOTE: *Cole slaw* (or *slaw*) is a popular salad made of shredded cabbage and mayonnaise.

YOU DO IT: *I'm so hungry that I'm going to order a side of..*

skip something (to) *v.* to decide against doing something.

example: I'm going to **skip** the salad today and just have a sandwich and a drink.

translation: I'm going to **decide against ordering** the salad today and just have a sandwich and a drink.

as spoken: I'm gonna **skip** the salad taday 'n just have a san'wich 'n a drink.

YOU DO IT: *I think I'd better skip dessert tonight because after lunch I...*

STUDENT BOOK (PRE-INTERMEDIATE)

AT THE RESTAURANT • *"Let's grab a bite!"*

sweet tooth (to have a) *v.* to have a passion for sweets.

example: Did you see all the candy Irene ate? She must really have a **sweet tooth**!

translation: Did you see all the candy Irene ate? She must really have a **passion for sweets**!

as spoken: Did 'ja see all the candy Irene ate? She must really have a **sweet tooth**!

YOU DO IT: *I think… has a sweet tooth because yesterday I saw him/her eat a…*

STREET TALK: *ESSENTIAL AMERICAN SLANG & IDIOMS*

REVIEW

THE GOOD, THE BAD, AND THE...

There were several slang terms and idioms in the first three lessons that were used to describe something either very good or very bad.

Write the number of the slang term or idiom in COLUMN A next to its matching picture in COLUMN B as well as next to the matching definition in COLUMN C.

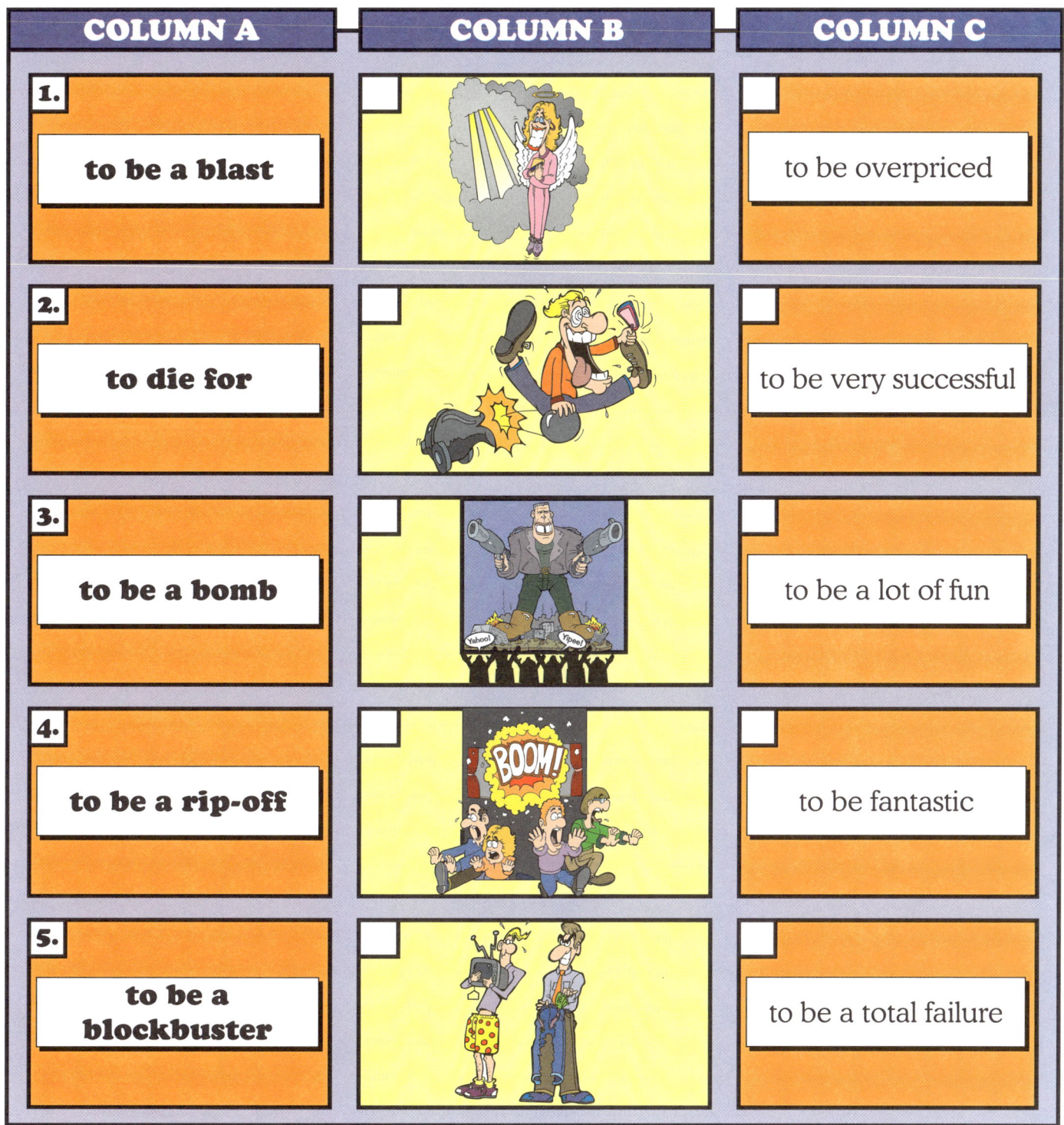

COLUMN A	COLUMN B	COLUMN C
1. to be a blast		to be overpriced
2. to die for		to be very successful
3. to be a bomb		to be a lot of fun
4. to be a rip-off		to be fantastic
5. to be a blockbuster		to be a total failure

STUDENT BOOK (PRE-INTERMEDIATE)

ON THE ROAD

"Let's go for a spin!"

GETTING STARTED — This lesson contains 14 new slang words & idioms.

A. MATCH THE PICTURES
Use the pictures to help you guess the meaning of the new slang words and expressions in the exercise on the opposite page.

STUDENT BOOK (PRE-INTERMEDIATE)

STREET TALK: *ESSENTIAL AMERICAN SLANG & IDIOMS*

READ THE SENTENCES AND CHECK THE BOX NEXT TO THE WORD OR PHRASE THAT BEST DEFINES THE SLANG OR IDIOM IN RED.

1. I drove over a nail and had a **blowout**.
   - ❏ flat tire
   - ❏ scratch on my car

2. My car was **totaled** in an accident. Now I have to buy a new one.
   - ❏ destroyed
   - ❏ slightly damaged

3. Yesterday a driver **ran a light** and almost hit me!
   - ❏ hit a light post
   - ❏ drove through a red light

4. Would you like to go for a **spin** in my new car?
   - ❏ drive
   - ❏ walk

5. I'm going to be late for work! I'd better **punch it**!
   - ❏ accelerate suddenly
   - ❏ stop suddenly

6. I was in a **fender-bender** today. The car repairs will be finished tomorrow.
   - ❏ minor car accident
   - ❏ major car accident

7. Yesterday, it took me an hour to drive home during **rush hour** and I only live a mile away!
   - ❏ the time when everyone is driving on the road
   - ❏ late hours

8. I'll be glad to drive you to the market. **Hop in**!
   - ❏ start jumping
   - ❏ get in

9. Bob got **hauled in** for speeding! He may have to spend the night in jail!
   - ❏ an award
   - ❏ arrested

10. The **bumper-to-bumper traffic** made me late!
    - ❏ light traffic
    - ❏ heavy traffic

11. The **cop** just arrested that man for bank robbery!
    - ❏ fire fighter
    - ❏ police officer

12. I ruined my tires when I drove over those **pot holes**.
    - ❏ rocks
    - ❏ deep holes in the street

13. I have to take the bus until my **clunker** gets fixed.
    - ❏ old bicycle
    - ❏ old car

14. I don't drive with Dan because he has a **lead foot**!
    - ❏ broken foot
    - ❏ tendency to drive fast

STUDENT BOOK (PRE-INTERMEDIATE)

ON THE ROAD • *"Let's go for a spin"*

DIALOGUE USING SLANG & IDIOMS

READ THE FOLLOWING DIALOGUE. CAN YOU UNDERSTAND ALL THE WORDS AND EXPRESSIONS IN RED?

John is showing Mark his new car.

Mark: Is this your new car? It's beautiful!

John: Thanks. It's sure a step up from the **clunker** I used to have. **Hop in** and I'll take you for a **spin**.

Mark: Just be careful. I know about your **lead foot** of yours. You don't want to get into a **fender-bender**! And you definitely don't want to get **hauled in** by a **cop** for speeding or **running a light**.

John: Don't worry. I promise I'm not going to **total my car** or get arrested my first day having a new car.

Mark: Okay, but be careful. The road to Nancy's house is full of **pot holes** and you don't want to get a **blowout**.

John: Don't worry! I'll take it slowly. Besides, since this is **rush hour**, we're not going to be able to go very fast with all the **bumper-to-bumper traffic**! But once it clears up, I'm going to **punch it**!

STUDENT BOOK (PRE-INTERMEDIATE)

STREET TALK: ESSENTIAL AMERICAN SLANG & IDIOMS

DIALOGUE USING STANDARD ENGLISH

FILL IN THE BLANKS BELOW TO COMPLETE THE TRANSLATION OF THE DIALOGUE FROM THE OPPOSITE PAGE.

John is showing Mark his new car.

Mark: Is this your new car? It's beautiful!

John: Thanks. It's sure a step up from the **old** _ _ _ I used to have. **Get** _ _ and I'll take you for a _ _ _ _ _ .

Mark: Just be careful. I know about your **tendency to drive** _ _ _ _ . You don't want to get into a **car** _ _ _ _ _ _ _ _ _ ! And you definitely don't want to get _ _ _ _ _ _ _ _ by a **police** _ _ _ _ _ _ _ for speeding or **driving through a red** _ _ _ _ _ .

John: Don't worry. I promise I'm not going to _ _ _ _ _ _ _ **my car** or get arrested my first day having a new car.

Mark: Okay, but be careful. The road to Nancy's house is full of **deep** _ _ _ _ _ and you don't want to get a _ _ _ _ **tire**.

John: Don't worry! I'll take it slowly. Besides, since this is **the hour when most of the cars are on the** _ _ _ _ , we're not going to be able to go very fast with all the **heavy** _ _ _ _ _ _ _ ! But once it clears up, I'm going to **accelerate** _ _ _ _ _ _ _ _ !

STUDENT BOOK (PRE-INTERMEDIATE)

ON THE ROAD • *"Let's go for a spin"*

THE SAME DIALOGUE USING "REAL SPEAK"

LISTENING

John's showing Mark 'is new car.

Mark: Is this yer new car? It's beaudiful!

John: Thanks. It's sher a step up fr'm the **clunker** I usta have. **Hop in** 'n a'll take ya fer a **spin**.

Mark: Jus' be careful. I know about yer **lead foot**. Ya don't wanna ged into a **fender-bender**! And ya definitely don't wanna get **hauled in** by a **cop** fer speeding 'r **running a light**.

John: Don't worry. I promise I'm not gonna **todal my car** 'r get arrested my firs' day having a new car.

Mark: Okay, but be careful. The road ta Nancy's house is full 'a **pot holes** 'n ya don't wanna ged a **blowout**.

John: Don't worry! A'll take it slowly. Besides, since this is **rush hour**, w'r not gonna be able da go very fast with all the **bumper-da-bumper traffic**! B't once it clears up, I'm gonna **punch it**!

A CLOSER LOOK AT "REAL SPEAK"

WANT TO = *WANNA*

RULE: When "want to" is followed by a verb, it is often shortened (or *reduced*) to **wanna**.

HOW DO WE GET FROM "WANT TO" TO WANNA?

I *want to go* for a spin.
⬇
I *wanXXo go* for a spin.
⬇
I *wan o go* for a spin.
⬇
I *wan o go* for a spin.
⬇
I *wanuh go* for a spin.
⬇
I **wanna** go for a spin.

In the phrase "want to," the hard sounds (or *full stop* sounds) of both "t's" disappear in everyday speech.

All unstressed short vowels (such as the *o* in "to" of *"want to"*) are commonly pronounced *uh* (often seen in the dictionary as the symbol: ə).

This shortened version of *"want to"* is so common that it has its own accepted spelling of: **wanna**.

STUDENT BOOK (PRE-INTERMEDIATE)

STREET TALK: *ESSENTIAL AMERICAN SLANG & IDIOMS*

WANTS TO = WANSTA

RULE: When "wants to" is followed by a verb, it is often shortened (or *reduced*) to **wansta**.

IN STANDARD ENGLISH	IN "REAL SPEAK"
I **want to** go for a spin.	I **wanna** go for a spin.
Do you **want to** hop in and go?	Do you **wanna** hop in and go?
We **want to** miss rush hour.	We **wanna** miss rush hour.
They **want to** sell their old clunker.	They **wanna** sell their old clunker.
He **wants to** avoid the pot holes.	He **wansta** avoid the pot holes.
She **wants to** grab a cab.	She **wansta** grab a cab.

PRACTICE USING "REAL SPEAK"

SPEAKING

PAIR WORK

A. WANNA OR WANSTA
Each person takes a turn asking a question from the left column. The other person answers with a sentence which includes the words in brackets from the right column. Don't forget to use *wanna* or *wansta*!

1. **PERSON A:** Do you want to take in a movie tonight?
   PERSON B: [Yes] [see] [comedy]

2. **PERSON A:** What does your brother want to do tonight?
   PERSON B: [He] [pig out] [pizza]

3. **PERSON A:** What do your friends want to order for dinner?
   PERSON B: [Everybody] [hamburgers] [side of fries]

4. **PERSON A:** Does Steve want to take home the leftovers?
   PERSON B: [Yes] [he] [doggie bag]

1. **PERSON B:** Do you want to take a drive in my new car?
   PERSON A: [Yes] [spin] [beach]

2. **PERSON B:** Where does your mother want to go for dinner?
   PERSON A: [She] [eat] [French restaurant]

3. **PERSON B:** Does anybody want to play cards tonight?
   PERSON A: [Nobody] [play cards] [watch TV]

4. **PERSON B:** Does the cat want to go outside?
   PERSON A: [No] [sleep] [sofa]

STUDENT BOOK (PRE-INTERMEDIATE)

ON THE ROAD • *"Let's go for a spin"*

PRACTICE THE VOCABULARY

LISTENING

B. CLOZE EXERCISE
Listen and complete the following conversation by writing the missing words you hear in the spaces provided.

Dick: Hey, Jack! I know it's _____, and there's _____ traffic all the way into town, but could you give me a ride to_____?

Jack: What happened to _____? Were you in another _____?

Dick: No, some guy with a _____ was speeding and _____ and _____ my old _____ last night!

Jack: That's terrible! Well, _____. I'd be glad to take you to work. Did the guy who hit your car get arrested?

Dick: He sure did. Luckily, there was a _____ nearby who _____.

Jack: Well, the most important thing is that you're okay.

LISTENING

C. USAGE MISTAKES
Listen to the sentences and decide if the slang and idioms are used correctly or incorrectly. Place a check mark in the appropriate box.

Sentence 1.	☐ CORRECT	☐ INCORRECT
Sentence 2.	☐ CORRECT	☐ INCORRECT
Sentence 3.	☐ CORRECT	☐ INCORRECT
Sentence 4.	☐ CORRECT	☐ INCORRECT
Sentence 5.	☐ CORRECT	☐ INCORRECT
Sentence 6.	☐ CORRECT	☐ INCORRECT
Sentence 7.	☐ CORRECT	☐ INCORRECT
Sentence 8.	☐ CORRECT	☐ INCORRECT

STUDENT BOOK (PRE-INTERMEDIATE)

STREET TALK: *ESSENTIAL AMERICAN SLANG & IDIOMS*

SPEAKING

D. BLANK BLANK - *(Part 1)*
Person A goes first / Person B turns to the top of the next page.
Person A: Read the sentence on the left with the blanks to Person B.
Person B should answer with the words from the right column.

PAIR WORK A

	PERSON A says...	PERSON B answers...
1.	It took me an hour to drive home because of all the [blank]-[blank]-[blank] [blank].	**bumper-to-bumper traffic**
2.	It's such a beautiful day. Let's put the top down and [blank] [blank] [blank] [blank] in my new sports car.	**go for a spin**
3.	That was really close! That driver didn't stop! He [blank] [blank] [blank] and almost hit us!	**ran a light**
4.	You drive too fast! Your just like your father. You have a [blank] [blank]!	**lead foot**
5.	We have to get to the hospital fast. The contractions are coming every minute! [blank] [blank]!!	**punch it**
6.	The car wasn't damaged too badly in the accident. It was just a little [blank]-[blank].	**fender-bender**
7.	I'm going to the market, too. [blank] [blank]. I'd be happy to give you a ride there.	**hop in**
8.	It looks like I'm going to have to buy a new car after the accident. My poor car was [blank].	**totaled**
9.	When are you going to get rid of that old [blank] and buy yourself a new car?	**clunker**

D. BLANK BLANK - *(Part 2)*
Listen to the sentences read by Person B. Replace the blanks with the best word(s) from the list below. Not all the words will be used!

WORD LIST
- ☐ totaled
- ☐ blowout
- ☐ clunker
- ☐ punch it
- ☐ cop
- ☐ pot holes
- ☐ hauled in
- ☐ go for a spin
- ☐ ran a light
- ☐ rush hour
- ☐ bumper-to-bumper traffic

STUDENT BOOK (PRE-INTERMEDIATE)

ON THE ROAD • *"Let's go for a spin"*

SPEAKING

D. BLANK BLANK - *(Part 1)*
Listen to the sentences read by Person A. Replace the blanks with the best word(s) from the list below. Not all the words will be used!

PAIR WORK B

WORD LIST
- ☐ totaled
- ☐ clunker
- ☐ hauled in
- ☐ go for a spin
- ☐ ran a light
- ☐ punch it
- ☐ fender-bender
- ☐ hop in
- ☐ lead foot
- ☐ rush hour
- ☐ bumper-to-bumper traffic

D. BLANK BLANK - *(Part 2)*
Person B, now it's your turn!
Person B: Read the sentence on the left with the blanks to Person A.
Person A should answer with the words from the right column.

	PERSON B says...	PERSON A answers...
1.	I had to buy a new tire this morning when I got a [blank] on the way to work.	blowout
2.	I'm sorry I'm so late. I was stuck in [blank]-[blank]-[blank] [blank] for the past hour.	bumper-to-bumper traffic
3.	My sister is a [blank]. Last week, she arrested two robbers!	cop
4.	I'm bored. Let's get out of this house for a while and [blank] [blank] [blank] [blank] in the neighborhood.	go for a spin
5.	Look at all the cars on the road! I hate driving during [blank] [blank]!	rush hour
6.	They really should fix these roads. They're so bumpy because of all the [blank] [blank].	pot holes
7.	John [blank] his father's car yesterday in an accident! Luckily, John wasn't hurt.	totaled
8.	It's a good thing there wasn't a cop around. You just [blank] [blank] [blank]!	ran a light
9.	Did you hear the news? Rob got [blank] [blank] for drunk driving!!	hauled in

STUDENT BOOK (PRE-INTERMEDIATE)

STREET TALK: ESSENTIAL AMERICAN SLANG & IDIOMS

VOCABULARY - A Closer Look

blowout *n.* a punctured tire. (said because the air "blows out" of the tire).

example: I was late to work because I got a **blowout** on the highway this morning.

translation: I was late to work because I got a **punctured tired** on the highway this morning.

as spoken: I w'z late ta work 'cuz I god a **blowoud** on the highway this morning.

SYNONYM: **flat** *n.* (short for: *flat tire*).

YOU DO IT: *My car got a blowout when I went to...*

bumper-to-bumper traffic *exp.* traffic that is so heavy that there is no room between cars.

example: It took me two hours to get home because of all the **bumper-to-bumper traffic**... and I only live a few miles from work!

translation: It took me two hours to get home because of all the **heavy traffic**... and I only live a few miles from work!

as spoken: It took me two hours ta get home because of all the **bumper-da-bumper traffic**... an' I only live a few miles fr'm work!

YOU DO IT: *The road to ...is famous for bumper-to-bumper traffic.*

clunker *n.* an old car in poor condition.

example: I finally sold my old **clunker** and bought a new Mercedes Benz!

translation: I finally sold my old **worn out car** and bought a new Mercedes Benz!

as spoken: I fin'lly sold my old **clunker** 'n bod a new Mercedes Benz!

SYNONYM: **jalopy** *n.*

YOU DO IT: *The last clunker I owned was a...*

STUDENT BOOK (PRE-INTERMEDIATE)

ON THE ROAD • *"Let's go for a spin"*

cop *n.* police officer (originally called a *copper*).

example: Be careful not to speed on this street. I just saw a **cop**.

translation: Be careful not to speed on this street. I just saw a **police officer**.

as spoken: Be careful not ta speed on this street. I jus' saw a **cop**.

NOTE: This popular term (used even among police officers) came from the days of gangsters when police officers were known for wearing a *copper* badge.

YOU DO IT: *The job of a cop is to...*

fender-bender *n.* a minor car accident.

example: I got into a car accident this morning, but don't worry. It was just a **fender-bender**.

translation: I got into a car accident this morning, but don't worry. It was just a **minor accident**.

as spoken: I god into a car accident this morning, b't don't worry. It w'z just a **fender-bender**.

YOU DO IT: *The last time I saw a fender-bender was...*

hauled in (to get) *exp.* to get taken to jail.

example: Did you hear the news? Jim got **hauled in** for drunk driving!

translation: Did you hear the news? Jim got **taken to jail** for drunk driving!

as spoken: Did 'ja hear the news? Jim got **hauled in** fer drunk driving!

YOU DO IT: *I've never been hauled in for...*

hop in (to) *v.* to enter a car.

example: I'd be happy to drive you to the grocery store this morning. **Hop in**!

translation: I'd be happy to drive you to the grocery store this morning. **Get in the car**!

as spoken: I'd be happy da drive you ta the groc'ry store this morning. **Hop in**!

YOU DO IT: *Hop in! I'd be glad to drive you to...*

STREET TALK: ESSENTIAL AMERICAN SLANG & IDIOMS

lead foot (to have a) *exp.* said of a driver who drives too fast as if his/her foot were made of lead, causing the car's accelerator pedal to be pressed all the way down.

example: My father got his third speeding ticket in two weeks! My mother is always yelling at him about his **lead foot**.

translation: My father got his third speeding ticket in two weeks! My mother is always yelling at him about his **tendency to drive fast**.

as spoken: My father god 'is third speeding ticket 'n two weeks! My mother's always yelling ad 'im aboud 'is **lead foot**.

YOU DO IT: My (family member or friend) has a lead foot!

pot hole *n.* a large hole in the street resembling the size and depth of a kitchen pot.

example: Unfortunately, the city doesn't have enough money to fix all the **pot holes**.

translation: Unfortunately, the city doesn't have enough money to fix all the **holes in the street**.

as spoken: Unfortunately, the cidy doesn' have anuf money da fix all the **pot holes**.

YOU DO IT: [Street name] has a lot of pot holes!

punch it (to) *exp.* to press the accelerator pedal down suddenly.

example: **Punch it**! We only have five minutes before the movie starts!

translation: **Accelerate immediately**! We only have five minutes before the movie starts!

as spoken: **Punch it**! We only have five minutes b'fore the movie starts!

YOU DO IT: We're late for.... Punch it!

run a light (to) *exp.* to go through the red light of a traffic signal.

example: Did you see that?! That guy **ran the light** and almost hit us!

translation: Did you see that?! That guy **went through the red light of the traffic signal** and almost hit us!

as spoken: Did 'ja see that?! That guy **ran the light** 'n almost hid us!

YOU DO IT: The danger in running a red light is...

STUDENT BOOK (PRE-INTERMEDIATE)

ON THE ROAD • *"Let's go for a spin"*

rush hour *n.* the time when most drivers are on the road at the same time (usually at the opening or close of business).

example: Let's meet for dinner tonight, but let's make it around seven o'clock. I don't want to drive during **rush hour**.

translation: Let's meet for dinner tonight, but let's make it around seven o'clock. I don't want to drive during **the time when most drivers are on the road at the same time**.

as spoken: Let's meet fer dinner danight, b't let's make id aroun' seven a'clock. I don't wanna drive during **rush hour**.

NOTE: This term is still commonly used although it's no longer accurate since in most big cities *rush hour* actually lasts for several hours!

YOU DO IT: *During rush hour, it takes me …hours to get to…*

spin (to take a) *exp.* to take a short drive with no particular destination.

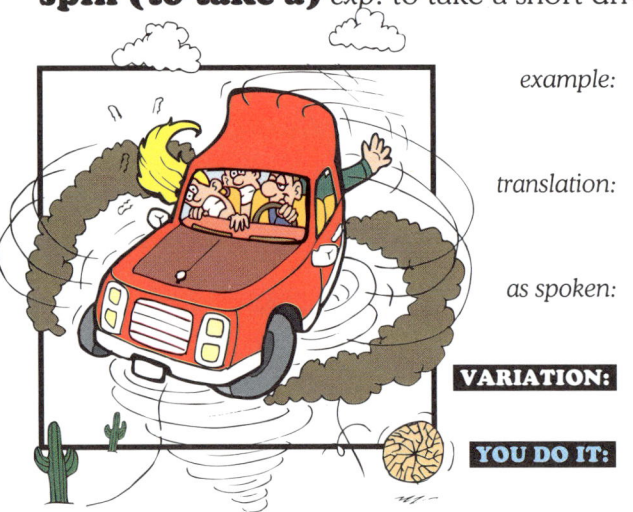

example: It's such a beautiful day! Why don't we **take a spin** in my new car?

translation: It's such a beautiful day! Why don't we **take a relaxing drive** in my new car?

as spoken: It's such a beaudif'l day! Why don' we **take a spin** 'n my new car?

VARIATION: **spin (to go for a)** *exp.*

YOU DO IT: *If I had a Porche, I'd ask …if he/she wanted to take a spin with me!*

total a car (to) *exp.* to completely destroy a car in an accident.

example: Did you hear the news? Dianne **totaled her car** in an accident last night! Luckily, no one was hurt.

translation: Did you hear the news? Dianne **destroyed her car** in an accident last night! Luckily, no one was hurt.

as spoken: Did 'ju hear the news? Dianne **toddled 'er car** in 'n accident las' night! Luckily, no one w'z hurt.

YOU DO IT: *If I total my father's new car, he will…*

88   STUDENT BOOK (PRE-INTERMEDIATE)

REVIEW

IN OTHER WORDS...SYNONYMS!

In the vocabulary section of previous lessons, you may have noticed that there are synonyms for many of the slang terms and idioms you've learned.
Write the number of the picture from COLUMN A next to its matching synonym in COLUMN B.

LESSON 8 — AT SCHOOL

"I had to pull an all-nighter!"

GETTING STARTED — This lesson contains **14** new slang words & idioms.

A. MATCH THE PICTURES
Use the pictures to help you guess the meaning of the new slang words and expressions in the exercise on the opposite page.

90   STUDENT BOOK (PRE-INTERMEDIATE)

STREET TALK: *ESSENTIAL AMERICAN SLANG & IDIOMS*

MATCH THE WORDS IN RED WITH THE BEST DEFINITION FROM THE RIGHT COLUMN. WRITE THE LETTER OF THE DEFINITION IN THE BOX.

1. Tony **cut class** yesterday and played outside instead.
2. My **psych** teacher is strange. I think she's neurotic!
3. I'm so excited! I **aced** the test!
4. I **pulled an all-nighter** studying for my math test!
5. The teacher surprised us all by giving us a **pop quiz**!
6. This class is too hard. I think I'm going to **drop it**.
7. My sister always gets **straight A's**.
8. If I don't pass the **final**, I'm going to be in big trouble!
9. I completely **blew** my exams.
10. What a **killer** test! It was really hard!
11. Paul **flunked** the course because he never studies.
12. I hope the teacher is giving **make-ups**.
13. You forgot about the test tomorrow? You'd better **cram** for it!
14. I passed the **mid-term**!

A. failed
B. psychology
C. perfect grades
D. surprise test
E. did extremely well on
F. mid-term examination
G. did poorly on
H. final examination
I. didn't attend class
J. stayed up all night
K. study hard in a short period of time
L. very difficult
M. second chances at taking the test
N. remove the class from my schedule

STUDENT BOOK (PRE-INTERMEDIATE)

AT SCHOOL • *"I had to pull an all-nighter!"*

DIALOGUE USING SLANG & IDIOMS

READ THE FOLLOWING DIALOGUE. CAN YOU UNDERSTAND ALL THE WORDS AND EXPRESSIONS IN RED?

Lee and David are talking about Eric.

David: I just heard Eric **flunked** our **psych** class! Is that true?

Lee: Yeah, I can't believe it. It's never happened to him before! He always gets **straight A's** on the **pop quizzes** and he even **aced** the **mid-term**. How could he possibly **blow** the **final**?

David: That's because he started to **cut class** all the time and stopped studying. I passed it because I **pulled an all nighter** trying to **cram** for it.

Lee: I've never taken such a **killer** test in my life. Unfortunately for Eric, the professor isn't allowing him to take a **make-up**.

David: He should have **dropped the class** when he had the chance!

STREET TALK: *ESSENTIAL AMERICAN SLANG & IDIOMS*

DIALOGUE USING STANDARD ENGLISH

CROSS OUT THE WORDS OR PHRASES THAT DO _NOT_ HAVE THE SAME MEANING AS THE SLANG TERMS OR IDIOMS FROM THE OPPOSITE PAGE.

Lee and David are talking about Eric.

David: I just heard Eric **(failed) (passed)** our **(physics) (psychology)** class! Is that true?

Lee: Yeah, I can't believe it. It's never happened to him before! He always gets **(perfect grades) (bad grades)** on the **(scary tests) (surprise tests)** and he even **(did poorly on) (did extremely well on)** the **(mid-term course) (mid-term examination)**. How could he possibly **(do better than me on) (do poorly on)** the **(final examination) (final day)**?

David: That's because he started to **(sleep in class) (miss class intentionally)** all the time and stopped studying. I passed it because I **(stayed up for several nights) (stayed up all night)** trying to **(study a little) (study hard)** for it.

Lee: I've never taken such a **(difficult) (easy)** test in my life. Unfortunately for Eric, the professor isn't allowing him to take **(a re-test) (his makeup to class)**.

David: He should have **(taken more classes) (removed the class from his schedule)** when he had the chance!

STUDENT BOOK (PRE-INTERMEDIATE)

AT SCHOOL • *"I had to pull an all-nighter!"*

THE SAME DIALOGUE USING "REAL SPEAK"

Lee 'n David 'er talking aboud Eric.

David: I just heard thad Eric **flunked** 'ar **psych** class! Izat true?

Lee: Yeah, I can't b'lieve it. It's never happened to 'im b'fore! He always gets **straid A's** on the **pop quizzes** an' 'e even **aced** the **mid-term**. How could 'e possibly **blow** the **final**?

David: That's 'cuz 'e starded da **cut class** all the time 'n stopped studying. I passed it 'cuz I **pulled 'n all nider** trying da **cram** for it.

Lee: I've never taken such a **killer** test in my life. Unfortunately fer Eric, the prafesser isn' allowing 'im to take a **make-up**.

David: He should 'a **dropped the class** when 'e had the chance!

A CLOSER LOOK AT "REAL SPEAK"

THE DISAPPEARING "H"

| he = 'e | him = 'im | his = 'is | her = 'er |

RULE: Often the "h" disappears from the pronouns "he," "him," "his," and "her" when they are not stressed in the sentence. However, the "h" is always pronounced when the pronoun is stressed or begins the sentence.

EXAMPLES:	NOTES:
What did **'e** say about the psych class? Look at **'im** cram for that test! Isn't that **'is** new bicycle? I think that's **'er** teacher.	The "h" is silent since in these examples, "he," "him," "his," and "her" are all unstressed and do not begin the sentence.
I like the class but **HE** doesn't. Don't tell me you're upset. Tell **HIM**. That's not my pencil. It's **HIS**. You invited **HER** to your party? **HE** left for college yesterday. **HER** cat ruined all the furniture.	The "h" is pronounced because in these examples, "he," "him," "his," and "her" are all stressed or begin the sentence.

STUDENT BOOK (PRE-INTERMEDIATE)

STREET TALK: *ESSENTIAL AMERICAN SLANG & IDIOMS*

THE DISAPPEARING "TH"

them = 'em

RULE: The "th" often disappears from the pronoun "them" when it is not stressed in the sentence. However, when "them" is stressed, the "th" is always pronounced. Note that the "real speak" pronunciation of "them" (**'em**) and "him" (**'im**) often sounds the same. The distinction lies in the context!

EXAMPLES:	NOTES:
He noticed three of **'em** standing on the corner. I don't like Cindy and Ron. I never talk to **'em**.	The *"th"* is silent since in these examples, "them" is unstressed.
I wasn't talking to you, I was talking to **THEM**! Don't give the money to me, give it to **THEM**!	The *"th"* is pronounced because in these examples, "them" is stressed.

PRACTICE USING "REAL SPEAK"

LISTENING

A. TWO MISSING WORDS
Listen to the sentences and write the missing words in the spaces below.

1. I talked [a]_____ [b]_____ last week [c]_____ [d]_____ said [e]_____ [f]_____ mother was coming to [g]_____ [h]_____ for the holidays.

2. What did Stacey [a]_____ [b]_____ friend, Stephanie, was going to do [c]_____ [d]_____ cat while she was away on vacation?

3. [a]_____ [b]_____ must have [c]_____ [d]_____ about the handsome guy and [e]_____ [f]_____ came [g]_____ [h]_____ apartment yesterday. He even brought flowers [i]_____ [j]_____ !

STUDENT BOOK (PRE-INTERMEDIATE)

AT SCHOOL • *"I had to pull an all-nighter!"*

PRACTICE THE VOCABULARY

LISTENING

B. TRUTH OR LIE
The students below are calling home. As you look at the thoughts of the students, decide whether or not they are telling the truth or a lie based on the conversation you hear.

STREET TALK: *ESSENTIAL AMERICAN SLANG & IDIOMS*

SPEAKING

C. PARAPHRASING - WHAT'S ANOTHER WAY TO SAY...? - *(Part 1)*
Person A goes first / Person B turns to the top of the next page.

Person A: Ask the following questions to Person B who will answer the questions using the slang and idioms just learned.

For fun: If Person B's answer is correct, say *"You hit the nail on the head!"* which means "You're right!" in slang.
If Person B's answer is *not* correct, say *"You're way off!"* which means "You made a mistake" in slang.

PERSON A	ANSWER
1. What's another word for "failed"?	**flunked**
2. What's another word for "difficult"?	**killer**
3. What's another way to say "stay up all night studying"?	**pull an all-nighter**
4. What do you call a "test taken in the middle of the term"?	**mid-term**
5. What do you call "the last big test for a class"?	**the final**
6. How do you say "to remove a class from one's schedule"?	**to drop a class**
7. How do you say "someone didn't attend class"?	**someone cut class**

C. PARAPHRASING - WHAT'S ANOTHER WAY TO SAY...? - *(Part 2)*
Person B will now ask you some questions. Answer the questions using one of the slang words or idioms from the box below. Not all the words will be used!

WORD LIST
- ☐ to cram
- ☐ to ace a test
- ☐ to blow a test
- ☐ pop quiz
- ☐ a make-up
- ☐ straight A's
- ☐ psych class
- ☐ killer

STUDENT BOOK (PRE-INTERMEDIATE)

AT SCHOOL • *"I had to pull an all-nighter!"*

C. PARAPHRASING - WHAT'S ANOTHER WAY TO SAY...? - *(Part 1)*
Person A will now ask you some questions. Answer the questions using one of the slang words or idioms from the box below. Not all the words will be used!

PAIR WORK B

WORD LIST
- ☐ mid-term
- ☐ to drop a class
- ☐ flunked
- ☐ pull an all nighter
- ☐ killer
- ☐ the final
- ☐ someone cut class
- ☐ psych class

C. PARAPHRASING - WHAT'S ANOTHER WAY TO SAY...? - *(Part 2)*
Person B, now it's your turn!

Person B: Ask the following questions to Person A who will answer the questions using the slang and idioms just learned.

For fun: If Person A's answer is correct, say *"You hit the nail on the head!"* which is slang for "You're right!"
If Person A's answer is *not* correct, say *"You're way off!"* which is slang for "You made a mistake."

PERSON A	ANSWER
1. What's another way to say "surprise test"?	pop quiz
2. What's another way to say "to study very hard"?	to cram
3. What do you call "a second chance at taking a test"?	a make-up
4. What's another way to say "psychology class"?	psych class
5. How do you say "to do extremely well on a test"?	to ace a test
6. How do you say "to do poorly on a test"?	to blow a test
7. What's another way to say "perfect grades"?	straight A's

98   STUDENT BOOK (PRE-INTERMEDIATE)

STREET TALK: ESSENTIAL AMERICAN SLANG & IDIOMS

VOCABULARY - A Closer Look

ace a test (to) *exp.* to do extremely well on a test.

example: I studied for weeks and weeks. I just know I'm going to **ace the test**!

translation: I studied for weeks and weeks. I just know I'm going to **do extremely well on the test**!

as spoken: I studied fer weeks 'n weeks. I jus' know I'm gonna **ace the test**!

YOU DO IT: *(Use "ace the test" in a sentence)*

blow a test (to) *exp.* to do poorly on a test.

example: Steve **blew the test** in algebra. I always thought he loved math!

translation: Steve **did poorly on the test** in algebra. I always thought he loved math!

as spoken: Steve **blew the test** 'n algebra. I always thod 'e loved math!

YOU DO IT: *(Use "blow the test" in a sentence)*

cram (to) *v.* to study very hard in a short period of time.

example: I should have been studying all week. Now I have to stay up and **cram** for this test tomorrow morning!

translation: I should have been studying all week. Now I have to stay up and **study hard** for this test tomorrow morning!

as spoken: I should'ev been studying all week. Now I hafta stay up 'n **cram** fer this tes' tamorrow morning!

YOU DO IT: *(Use "cram" in a sentence)*

STUDENT BOOK (PRE-INTERMEDIATE)

AT SCHOOL • *"I had to pull an all-nighter!"*

---

cut class (to) *exp.* to miss class intentionally.

example: I don't want to go to school. Let's **cut class** today and go to the movies.

translation: I don't want to go to school. Let's **miss class intentionally** today and go to the movies.

as spoken: I don' wanna go da school. Let's **cut class** taday 'n go da the movies.

YOU DO IT: *(Use "cut class" in a sentence)*

drop a class (to) *exp.* to remove a class from one's schedule.

example: You're taking eight classes this term? If you want any free time, you're going to have to **drop a class**... maybe two!

translation: You're taking eight classes this term? If you want any free time, you're going to have to **remove a class from your schedule**... maybe two!

as spoken: Y'r taking eight classes this term? If ya wan' any free time, y'r gonna hafta **drop a class**... maybe two!

YOU DO IT: *(Use "drop a class" in a sentence)*

final *n.* the final test which covers everything learned during the school term.

example: I need to study all week. If I don't pass the **final**, I won't be able to graduate!

translation: I need to study all week. If I don't pass the **final test covering everything we learned**, I won't be able to graduate!

as spoken: I need da study all week. If I don't pass the **final**, I won't be able da graduate!

YOU DO IT: *(Use "final" in a sentence)*

flunk (to) *v.* to fail a test or a subject.

example: I studied all night for this test! How could I have possibly flunked?

translation: I studied all night for this test! How could I have possibly failed?

as spoken: I studied all night fer this test! How could I'ev possibly **flunked**?

YOU DO IT: *(Use "flunk" in a sentence)*

STUDENT BOOK (PRE-INTERMEDIATE)

killer *adj.* • **1.** extremely difficult • **2.** terrific.

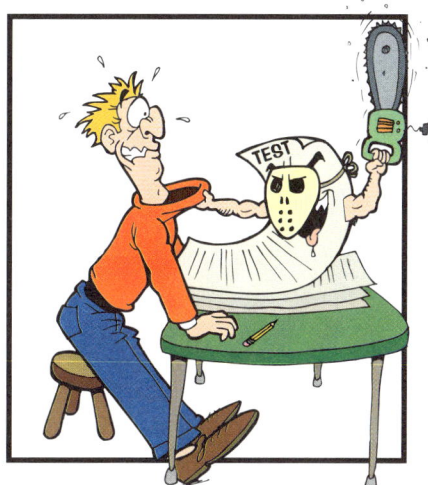

example -1: That was a **killer** test! I hope I didn't blow it!
translation: That was a **really difficult** test! I hope I didn't blow it!
as spoken: That w'z a **killer** test! I hope I didn't blow it!
example -2: That's a **killer** dress! Where did you buy it?
translation: That's a **terrific** dress! Where did you buy it?
as spoken: That's a **killer** dress! Where'd 'ja buy it?

NOTE: The difference between definitions **1.** and **2.** simply depends on the context.

YOU DO IT: *(Use "killer" in a sentence)*

make-up / make-up test *n.* a test that can be taken again at a later time, a re-test.

example: I was sick the day the teacher gave the class the test. Luckily she's giving **make-ups**.
translation: I was sick the day the teacher gave the class the test. Luckily she's giving **a second chance to take it**.
as spoken: I w'z sick the day the teacher gave the class the test. Luckily she's giving **make-ups**.

YOU DO IT: *(Use "make-up" in a sentence)*

mid-term *n.* a test taken in the middle of the term which covers all the material learned up to that point.

example: If I pass the biology **mid-term**, the rest of the course will be easy!
translation: If I pass the biology **test taken in the middle of the term**, the rest of the course will be easy!
as spoken: If I pass the bio **mid-term**, the rest 'a the course'll be easy!

YOU DO IT: *(Use "mid-term" in a sentence)*

pop quiz *n.* a surprise test (for which the student isn't able to study in advance).

example: My English teacher gave us a **pop quiz** today. Luckily I read all of the material last week!
translation: My English teacher gave us a **surprise test** today. Luckily I read all of the material last week!
as spoken: My English teacher gave us a **pop quiz** taday. Luckily I read all 'a the material last week!

YOU DO IT: *(Use "pop quiz" in a sentence)*

STUDENT BOOK (PRE-INTERMEDIATE)

ON THE ROAD • *"Let's go for a spin"*

psych *n.* a common shortened name for "psychology."

example: I have to hurry. My **psych** class starts in five minutes and I don't want to be late!

translation: I have to hurry. My **psychology** class starts in five minutes and I don't want to be late!

as spoken: I hafta hurry. My **psych** class starts 'n five minutes 'n I don't wanna be late!

NOTE: Many other school courses have shortened names such as:

bio	=	biology
chem	=	chemistry
econ	=	economy
English lit	=	English literature
home ec	=	home economics
math	=	mathematics
P.E. or phys ed	=	physical education
poli sci	=	political science
"sosh"	=	sociology
trig	=	trigonometry

YOU DO IT: *(Use "psych" in a sentence)*

pull an all-nighter (to) *exp.* to stay up all night studying.

example: I'm exhausted. I **pulled an all-nighter** studying for my chemistry final.

translation: I'm exhausted. I **stayed up all night** studying for my chemistry final.

as spoken: I'm exhausted. I **pulled 'n all-nider** studying fer my chemistry final.

YOU DO IT: *(Use "pull an all-nighter" in a sentence)*

straight A's *exp.* perfect grades (in all subjects or all of one's exams).

example: Did you see Nancy's report card? She got **straight A's** for the third time!

translation: Did you see Nancy's report card? She got **perfect grades** for the third time!

as spoken: Did 'ja see Nancy's report card? She got **straid A's** fer the third time!

YOU DO IT: *(Use "straight A's" in a sentence)*

STREET TALK: *ESSENTIAL AMERICAN SLANG & IDIOMS*

REVIEW

A FUN TIME WAS HAD BY ALL

Below are some slang terms and idioms you learned in previous lessons that are used to describe something fun to do in your free time.

Write the number of the slang term or idiom in COLUMN A next to its matching picture in COLUMN B as well as next to the matching definition in COLUMN C.

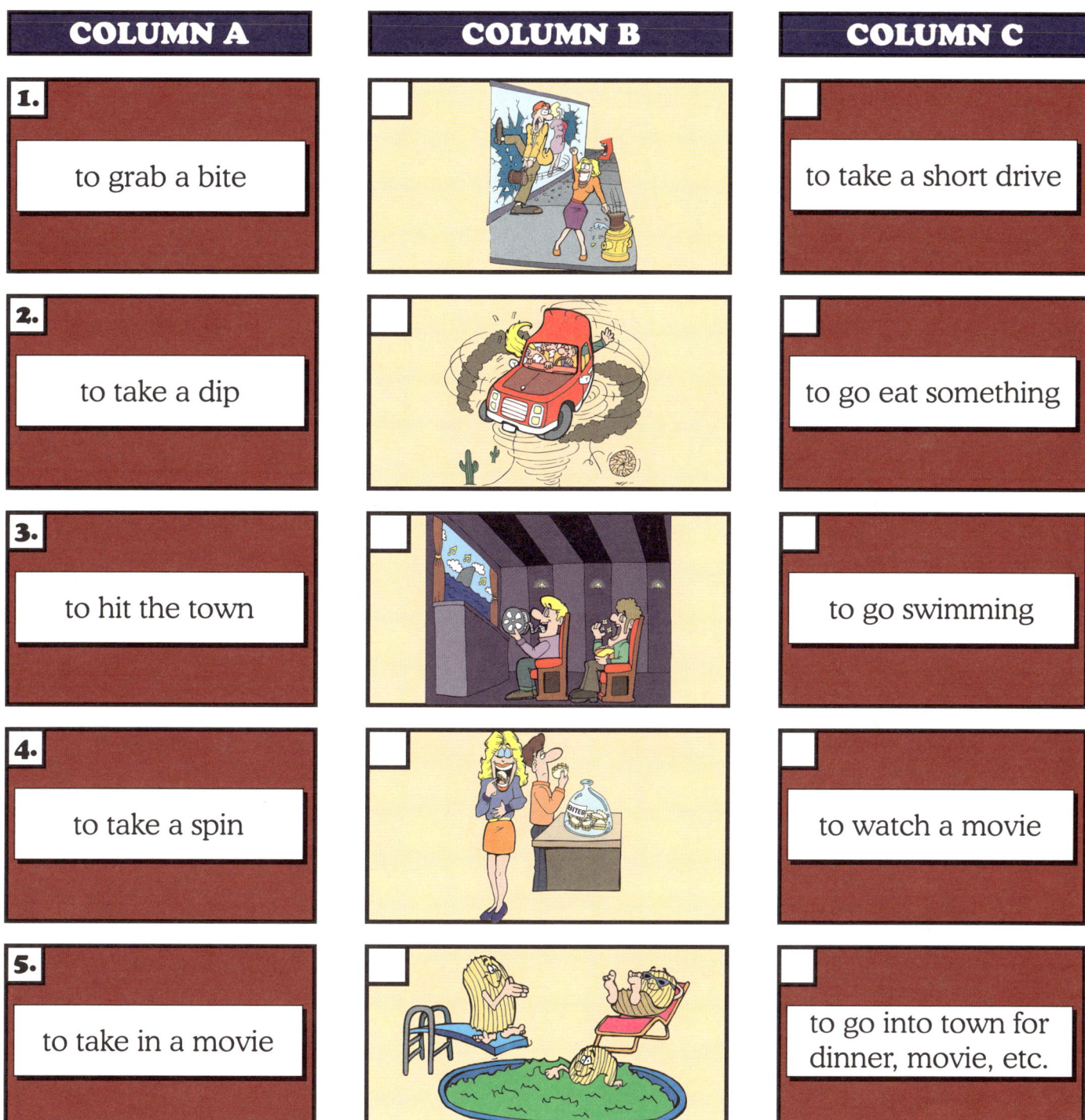

STUDENT BOOK (PRE-INTERMEDIATE) 103

LESSON 9
TO YOUR HEALTH
"I'm feeling under the weather"

GETTING STARTED — This lesson contains **14** new slang words & idioms.

A. **MATCH THE PICTURES**
Use the pictures to help you guess the meaning of the new slang words and expressions in the exercise on the opposite page.

STREET TALK: *ESSENTIAL AMERICAN SLANG & IDIOMS*

READ THE SENTENCES AND CHECK THE BOX NEXT TO THE WORD OR PHRASE THAT BEST DEFINES THE SLANG OR IDIOM IN RED.

1. You're warm. Are you **running a fever**?
   - ❏ feverish
   - ❏ feeling energetic

2. It takes weeks to **bounce back** from the flu.
   - ❏ recover
   - ❏ to get sick again

3. Joan got dizzy and almost **passed out**.
   - ❏ woke up
   - ❏ fainted

4. I missed three weeks of work because I was **sick as a dog**.
   - ❏ feeling great
   - ❏ feeling very sick

5. After being sick for a week, I'm finally back **in the pink**.
   - ❏ in good health
   - ❏ in poor health

6. There's nothing to do here. I'm **bored out of my mind**!
   - ❏ very bored
   - ❏ very excited

7. Don't work so hard. **Take it easy**!
   - ❏ relax
   - ❏ eat something

8. If I don't get out of this house, I'll **go stir crazy**!
   - ❏ go to sleep
   - ❏ become very restless from confinement

9. After a week of rest, you should be **raring to go**!
   - ❏ full of energy
   - ❏ exhausted

10. I can't sleep. I'm too **antsy**.
    - ❏ happy
    - ❏ nervous and agitated

11. Did your mother **pull through** after surgery?
    - ❏ get much worse
    - ❏ survive

12. You don't look well. Are you feeling **under the weather** today?
    - ❏ ill
    - ❏ healthy

13. There is no cure for a cold. You just have to let it **run its course**.
    - ❏ get better fast
    - ❏ lose strength on its own

14. I don't know what's wrong with me today. I don't really feel sick... just a little **blah**.
    - ❏ tired and lifeless
    - ❏ lively

STUDENT BOOK (PRE-INTERMEDIATE)

TO YOUR HEALTH • *"I'm feeling under the weather"*

DIALOGUE USING SLANG & IDIOMS

READ THE FOLLOWING DIALOGUE. CAN YOU UNDERSTAND ALL THE WORDS AND EXPRESSIONS IN RED?

Karen and Janet are talking on the phone.

Karen: Hi, Janet. I haven't heard from you in a while. How are you?

Janet: I've been **feeling under the weather**. I felt **blah** all morning then by the afternoon, I was **sick as a dog**. I started **running a fever** and actually thought I was going to **pass out**! Finally I had Brad take me to the doctor who said it was just a bad case of the flu which just has to **run its course**. I should be **raring to go** soon.

Karen: Well, it sounds like you'll definitely **pull through**. It takes a while to **bounce back** after having the flu, but I'm sure you'll be back **in the pink** soon. Just try to **take it easy** for a while.

Janet: You're right but I'm too **antsy** to just lie in bed. I get **bored out of my mind**.

Karen: I know what you mean. The last time I was sick, I started to **go stir crazy**!

STREET TALK: ESSENTIAL AMERICAN SLANG & IDIOMS

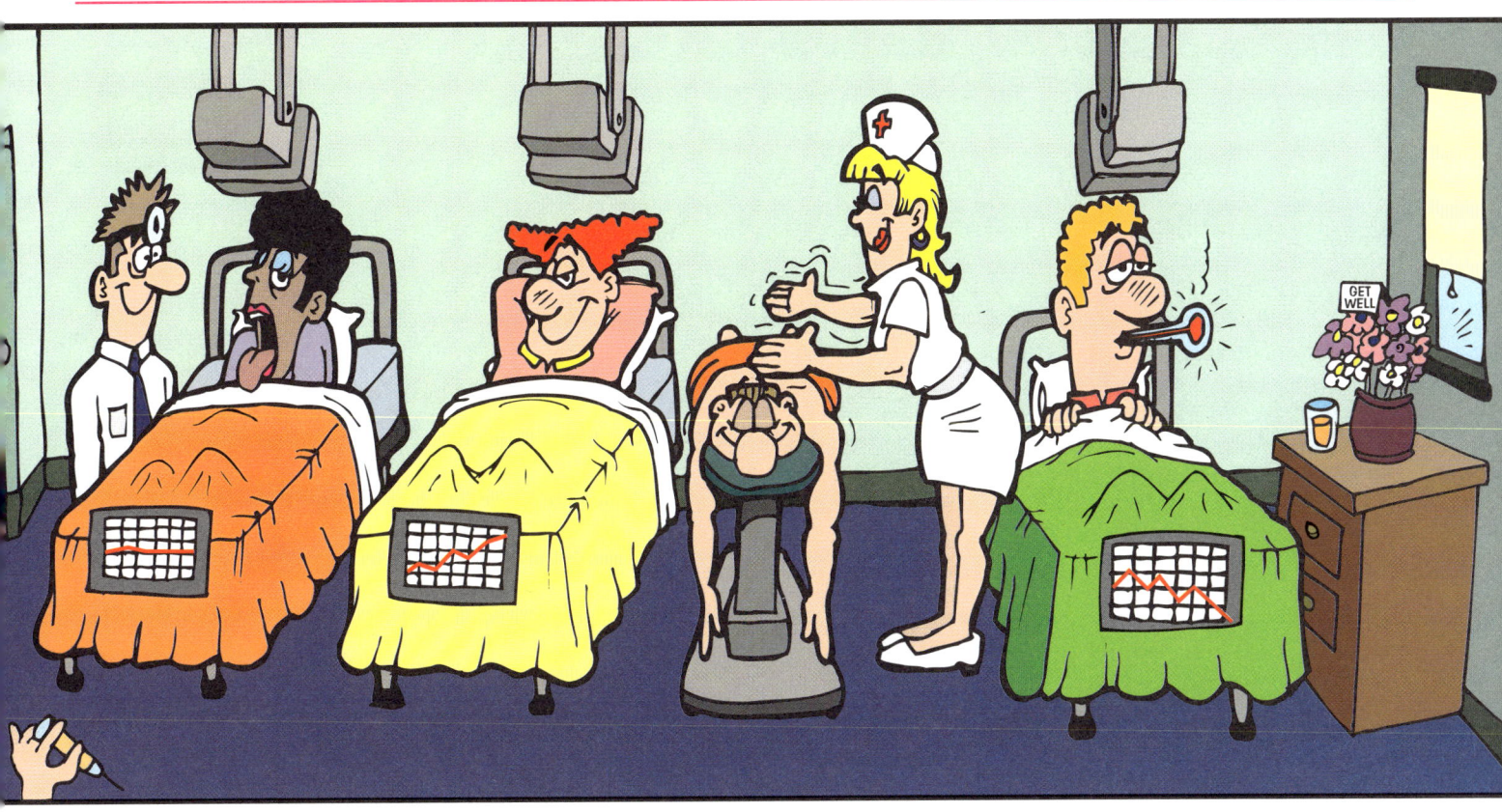

DIALOGUE USING STANDARD ENGLISH

CROSS OUT THE WORDS OR PHRASES THAT DO *NOT* HAVE THE SAME MEANING AS THE SLANG TERMS OR IDIOMS FROM THE OPPOSITE PAGE.

Karen and Janet are talking on the phone.

Karen: Hi, Janet. I haven't heard from you in a while. How are you?

Janet: I've been **(feeling great) (feeling sick)**. I felt **(energetic) (lifeless)** all morning then by the afternoon, I was **(extremely sick) (very happy)**. I started **(getting a fever) (jogging)** and actually thought I was going to **(faint) (leave)**! Finally I had Brad take me to the doctor who said it was just a bad case of the flu which just has to **(lose strength on its own) (get worse)**. I should be **(full of energy) (tired)** soon.

Karen: Well, it sounds like you'll definitely **(survive) (get worse)**. It takes a while to **(sleep) (recuperate)** after having the flu, but I'm sure you'll be back **(in good health) (in poor health)** soon. Just try to **(relax) (exercise)** for a while.

Janet: You're right but I'm too **(restless) (sleepy)** to just lie in bed. I get **(extremely bored) (a little bored)**.

Karen: I know what you mean. The last time I was sick, I started to **(become very restless from being confined to one place) (go crazy from being outside too much)**!

STUDENT BOOK (PRE-INTERMEDIATE)   **107**

TO YOUR HEALTH • *"I'm feeling under the weather"*

THE SAME DIALOGUE USING "REAL SPEAK"

Karen 'n Janet'er talking on the phone.

Karen: Hi, Janet. I haven't heard fr'm you in a while. How are ya?

Janet: I've been **feeling under the weather**. I felt **blah** all morning then by the afternoon, I w'z **sick as a dog**. I starded **running a fever** 'n akshelly thod I w'z gonna **pass out**! Fin'lly I had Brad take me da the doctor who said it w'z just a bad case 'a the flu which just hasta **run its course**. I should be **rarin' da go** soon.

Karen: Well, it sounds like you'll definitely **pull through**. It takes a while da **bounce back** after having the flu, bud I'm sher you'll be back **'n the pink** soon. Jus' try da **take id easy** fer a while.

Janet: Y'r right bud I'm too **antsy** da jus' lie 'n bed. I get **bored oudda my mind**!

Karen: I know what'cha mean. The las' time I w'z sick, I starded ta **go stir crazy**!

A CLOSER LOOK AT "REAL SPEAK"

YOU = YA

| you = ya | your = yer | you're = y'r | yours = yers |

RULE: Often the vowel combination "ou" in "you," "your," "you're," and "yours" is reduced as shown above. Note that "your" and "you're" are pronounced the same and are only differentiated by context.

STANDARD ENGLISH	"REAL SPEAK"
Do **you** feel blah today?	Do **ya** feel blah today?
You look a little under the weather.	**Ya** look a little under the weather.
Is that **your** sister?	Is that **yer** sister?
Your flu has to run its course.	**Yer** flu has to run its course.
You're my best friend	**Y'r** my best friend
You're right!	**Y'r** right!
Is that dog **yours**?	Is that dog **yers**?
I love my car, but **yours** is my favorite.	I love my car, but **yers** is my favorite.

STUDENT BOOK (PRE-INTERMEDIATE)

STREET TALK: ESSENTIAL AMERICAN SLANG & IDIOMS

PRACTICE USING "REAL SPEAK"

LISTENING EXERCISE

LISTENING

A. UNSCRAMBLE
Listen to the sentences in "real speak." Unscramble the word tiles and write each sentence you hear using standard English.

GOING YOU BIRTHDAY DO TO YOUR ARE FOR ? WHAT

1. Whaddya gonna do fer yer birthday

ARE SAY DID YOU GOING YOU TO ? HOUSE MOTHER'S YOUR

2. D'ja say yer gonna stay at yer mother's house?

YOUR EUROPE WANT ME . YOU TOLD IN STUDY TO FRIEND

3.

YOU BEST KNOW MY YOU ARE . FRIEND

4.

CAR WASHED TO GET TODAY YOU ARE GOING ? YOUR

5.

I'M WHERE TO THIS GOING . ? BALI SUMMER ARE GOING YOU

6.

STUDENT BOOK (PRE-INTERMEDIATE) 109

TO YOUR HEALTH • *"I'm feeling under the weather"*

PRACTICE THE VOCABULARY

LISTENING

B. THE FADING CONVERSATION
Listen to the conversations which are only partially shown on the page. Keep listening until the end of the dialogue then fill in the last line with your own words in response to what you've just heard.

Angela: Would you like to go to the movies tonight?
Jodi: I'd like to but I've been *feeling a little under the weather*. Maybe I'd better just stay home.
Angela: But won't you go *stir crazy*? Are you sure you d
Jodi: _____

Steve: Where have you been? I haven't seen you at school.
Al: I was *sick as a dog*. I was *running a high fever* all week!
Steve: Well, I hope it's already ru
Al: _____

Kim: I can't stand biology class. I don't know how I'm going to be able to dissect frogs today. I hope I don't get dizzy and *pass out*!
Doug: Just *take it easy*. You'll *pull through* just fine.
Kim: What about you? I heard that you g
Doug: _____

Nick: The doctor said you have to *take it easy* until the flu *runs its course*.
Tessa: But I'm so *antsy* being inside all day! I'm *bored out of my mind*!
Nick: Just think of all the things you'll
Tessa: _____

Carl: Good to see you again. Have you *bounced back* from that virus?
Sandy: Yeah, I'm feeling much better. I was *going stir crazy* lying in bed all day long. I hope you didn't catch it.
Carl: Now that you mention it, I am feelin
Sandy: _____

110

STUDENT BOOK (PRE-INTERMEDIATE)

SPEAKING

C. LIGHTS! CAMERA! ACTION!
Find a partner and choose one of the situations below. Create a dialogue using the slang and idioms given. Next, practice and perform your scene.

ROLE PLAY

SCENE 1. "Doctor & Patient"
Words to be used in this scene:

DOCTOR	PATIENT
☐ run its course	☐ blah
☐ in the pink	☐ headache
☐ plenty of rest	☐ coughing
☐ sleep	☐ sick as a dog

SCENE 2. "Two Friends"
Words to be used in this scene:

FRIEND #1	FRIEND #2
☐ under the weather	☐ raring to go
☐ stir crazy	☐ pull through
☐ tired	☐ aspirin
☐ runny nose	☐ go to bed

SCENE 3. "Boss & Employee"
Words to be used in this scene:

BOSS	EMPLOYEE
☐ in the pink	☐ pass out
☐ take it easy	☐ antsy
☐ go home	☐ feel terrible
☐ see a doctor	☐ watch TV

SCENE 4. "Parent & Child"
Words to be used in this scene:

PARENT	CHILD
☐ in the pink	☐ sick as a dog
☐ bounce back	☐ stay home
☐ liquids	☐ take it easy
☐ chicken soup	☐ read a book

SCENE 5. "Pharmacist & Client"
Words to be used in this scene:

PHARMACIST	CLIENT
☐ pull through	☐ a cold
☐ take it easy	☐ in the pink
☐ vitamin C	☐ blah
☐ eat right	☐ bored out of my mind

SCENE 6. "Nurse & Student"
Words to be used in this scene:

NURSE	STUDENT
☐ stir crazy	☐ antsy
☐ bounce back	☐ pass out
☐ temperature	☐ go home
☐ lie down	☐ dizzy

STUDENT BOOK (PRE-INTERMEDIATE)

TO YOUR HEALTH • *"I'm feeling under the weather"*

SPEAKING

D. TIC-TAC-TOE PAIR WORK

STEP ONE: Choose any 9 words or expressions from the word box below and write one in each colored square.

STEP TWO: Take turns choosing a definition to read to your partner. If the definition matches the words in one of your colored squares, make an "X" in the space provided.

GOAL: The first person to get 3 in a row, wins!

WORDS AND EXPRESSIONS FOR STEP ONE

under the weather	run its course	take it easy
feel blah	raring to go	antsy
sick as a dog	pull through	bored out of one's mind
run a fever	bounce back	stir crazy
pass out	in the pink	

DEFINITIONS FOR STEP TWO

- ☐ sick
- ☐ lifeless
- ☐ extremely sick
- ☐ getting a fever
- ☐ faint
- ☐ lose strength on its own
- ☐ full of energy
- ☐ survive
- ☐ recuperate
- ☐ in good health
- ☐ relax
- ☐ restless
- ☐ extremely bored
- ☐ crazy from being confined to one place

112 STUDENT BOOK (PRE-INTERMEDIATE)

VOCABULARY - A Closer Look

antsy (to be) *adj.* to be restless.

example: The movie was three hours long. After two hours, I started getting **antsy**.

translation: The movie was three hours long. After two hours, I started getting **restless**.

as spoken: The movie w'z three hours long. After two hours, I starded gedding **antsy**.

SYNONYM: ants in one's pants (to have) *exp.*

NOTE: Both expressions conjure up an image of ants crawling all over someone causing that person to move around and fidget.

YOU DO IT: *(Ask a question using "antsy")*

blah (to feel) *adj.* to feel lifeless, generally a little tired and unfocused.

example: Thank you for inviting me to go with you, but I think I'm going to just stay home tonight. I'm feeling a little **blah**.

translation: Thank you for inviting me to go with you, but I think I'm going to just stay home tonight. I'm feeling a little **tired and unfocused**.

as spoken: Thanks fer inviding me da go with you, b'd I think I'm gonna jus' stay home tanight. I'm feeling a liddle **blah**.

SYNONYM -1: out of it (to feel) *exp.*

SYNONYM -2: out of sorts (to feel) *exp.*

SYNONYM -3: to be oneself (not) *exp.*

YOU DO IT: *(Ask a question using "blah")*

bored out of one's mind (to be) *exp.* to be very bored.

example: I was **bored out of my mind** during the lecture! I couldn't wait for it to end!

translation: I was **terribly bored** during the lecture! I couldn't wait for it to end!

as spoken: I w'z **bored oudda my min'** during the lecture! I couldn't wait for it ta end!

SYNONYM -1: bored out of one's skull (to be) *exp.*

SYNONYM -2: bored stiff (to be) *exp.*

YOU DO IT: *(Ask a question using "bored out of one's mind")*

TO YOUR HEALTH • *"I'm feeling under the weather"*

bounce back (to) *v.* to recuperate.

example: Joanne is taking a long time to **bounce back** from the flu. She must be really sick.

translation: Joanne is taking a long time to **recuperate** from the flu. She must be really sick.

as spoken: Joanne's taking a long time da **bounce back** fr'm the flu. She mus' be really sick.

YOU DO IT: *(Ask a question using "bounce back")*

in the pink (to be) *exp.* to be experiencing good health (since the skin has a healthy pink color).

example: My grandmother is feeling much better. She's finally **in the pink** again.

translation: My grandmother is feeling much better. She's finally **experiencing good health** again.

as spoken: My gran'ma's feeling much bedder. She's fin'lly **in the pink** again.

YOU DO IT: *(Ask a question using "in the pink")*

pass out (to) *v.* to faint.

example: Dan **passed out** after working out at the gym. I think he exercised too hard!

translation: Dan **fainted** after working out at the gym. I think he exercised too hard!

as spoken: Dan **passed oud** after working oud at the gym. I think 'e exercised too hard!

YOU DO IT: *(Ask a question using "pass out")*

pull through (to) *v.* to survive.

example: Don't worry. I'm sure Debbie will **pull through**. The doctors say she's getting better every day.

translation: Don't worry. I'm sure Debbie will **survive**. The doctors say she's getting better every day.

as spoken: Don't worry. I'm sher Debbie'll pull through. The docters say she's gedding bedder ev'ry day.

SYNONYM: **make it (to)** *exp.*

YOU DO IT: *(Ask a question using "pull through")*

raring to go (to be) *exp.* to be energetic and ready to do something.

example: I know you feel blah right now but after a good night's sleep, I'm sure you'll be **raring to go**!

translation: I know you feel blah right now but after a good night's sleep, I'm sure you'll be **energetic and ready to do something**!

as spoken: I know ya feel blah right now bud after a good night's sleep, I'm sher you'll be **rarin' da go**!

NOTE: In this expression, the verb *raring* is almost always reduced to *rarin'*. It would actually sound strange to the ear to hear a speaker *not* use this reduction!

SYNONYM: **up and at them (to be)** *exp.*

NOTE: This expression is almost always reduced to: **to be up 'n ad 'em**.

YOU DO IT: *(Ask a question using "raring to go")*

run a fever (to) *exp.* to have a high body temperature, to be feverish.

example: If you start to **run a fever**, you should go see your doctor right away.

translation: If you start to **get a high body temperature**, you should go see your doctor right away.

as spoken: If ya start ta **run a fever**, ya should go see yer docter ride away.

YOU DO IT: *(Ask a question using "run a fever")*

run its course (to) *exp.* said of an illness that needs to lose strength on its own over time.

example: Unfortunately, there's no treatment for the common cold yet. It just has to **run its course**.

translation: Unfortunately, there's no treatment for the common cold yet. It just has to **lose strength on its own over time**.

as spoken: Unfortunately, there's no treatment fer the common cold yet. It just hasta **run its course**.

YOU DO IT: *(Ask a question using "run its course")*

sick as a dog (to be as) *exp.* to be extremely sick.

example: Usually I never get sick. But last week I was **sick as a dog**! Luckily, I'm doing a lot better now.

translation: Usually I never get sick. But last week I was **extremely sick**! Luckily, I'm doing a lot better now.

as spoken: Ujally I never get sick. B't last week I w'z **sick 'ez a dog**! Luckily, I'm doing a lot bedder now.

YOU DO IT: *(Ask a question using "sick as a dog")*

TO YOUR HEALTH • *"I'm feeling under the weather"*

stir crazy (to go) *exp.* to become very restless from being confined to one place.

example: I wish it would stop raining so we could go outside. I'm going to **go stir crazy**!

translation: I wish it would stop raining so we could go outside. I'm going to **become very restless from being confined to one place**!

as spoken: I wish it'd stop raining so we could go outside. I'm gonna **go stir crazy**!

YOU DO IT: *(Ask a question using "stir crazy")*

take it easy (to) *exp.* to relax.

example: If you don't **take it easy**, you're going to get sick from working so hard.

translation: If you don't **relax**, you're going to get sick from working so hard.

as spoken: If ya don't **take id easy**, y'r gonna get sick fr'm working so hard.

YOU DO IT: *(Ask a question using "take it easy")*

under the weather (to feel) *exp.* to feel sick.

example: Hi, Richard. You look a little tired today. Have you been **feeling under the weather**?

translation: Hi, Richard. You look a little tired today. Have you been **feeling sick**?

as spoken: Hi, Richard. You look a liddle tired taday. Have you been **feeling under the weather**?

YOU DO IT: *(Ask a question using "feel under the weather")*

REVIEW

THE NIGHT SHIFT

Below are some slang terms and idioms you learned in previous lessons that are used to describe something that happens at night.

Write the number of the slang term or idiom in COLUMN A next to its matching picture in COLUMN B as well as next to the matching definition in COLUMN C.

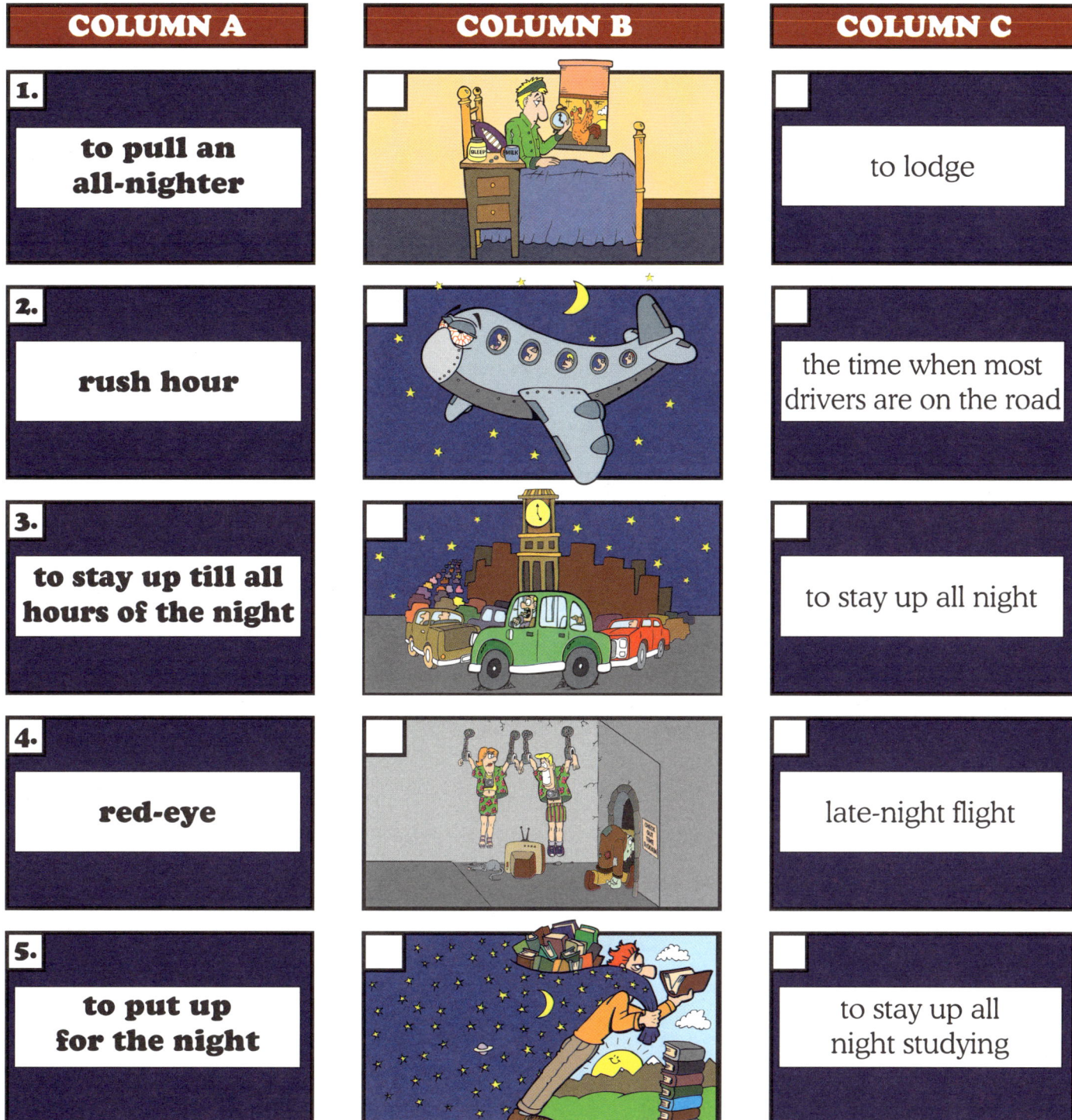

LESSON 10
ON A DATE
"He stood me up!"

GETTING STARTED — This lesson contains **15** new slang words & idioms.

A. MATCH THE PICTURES
Use the pictures to help you guess the meaning of the new slang words and expressions in the exercise on the opposite page.

STREET TALK: *ESSENTIAL AMERICAN SLANG & IDIOMS*

DECIDE IF THE DEFINITION GIVEN FOR THE WORDS IN RED IS TRUE OR FALSE.

1. They're not old enough to know true love. It's just **puppy love**.
   Definition: "immature love"
   ❑ True   ❑ False

2. Cathy's smiling at you. Maybe she has a **crush on** you!
   Definition: "infatuation for"
   ❑ True   ❑ False

3. That's your wife? When did you **tie the knot**?
   Definition: "get married"
   ❑ True   ❑ False

4. There are **no strings attached** to my invitation. I don't expect anything in return.
   Definition: "no hidden motives"
   ❑ True   ❑ False

5. If you don't want to go out with Bill, **turn him down**.
   Definition: "decline his offer"
   ❑ True   ❑ False

6. John is definitely not a hunk. He's the biggest **nerd**!
   Definition: "unexciting man"
   ❑ True   ❑ False

7. My boyfriend **dumped** me for another girl!
   Definition: "rejected"
   ❑ True   ❑ False

8. Ted was late, but he finally **showed up**.
   Definition: "appeared"
   ❑ True   ❑ False

9. I waited an hour for him. He **stood me up**!
   Definition: "never arrived"
   ❑ True   ❑ False

10. When I met your father, it was **love at first sight**.
    Definition: "love immediately"
    ❑ True   ❑ False

11. Yumiko is **drop-dead gorgeous**! Is she a model?
    Definition: "very beautiful"
    ❑ True   ❑ False

12. Leonard and I planned on having dinner together last night, but he had **to break our date**.
    Definition: "to cancel our date"
    ❑ True   ❑ False

13. If you don't really like Martin, don't go out with him. You're just **leading him on**!
    Definition: "making him falsely think you're interested in him"
    ❑ True   ❑ False

14. If you want a date with Jennifer, just **ask her out**!
    Definition: "ask her for a date"
    ❑ True   ❑ False

15. I've never met him before. It was a **blind date**.
    Definition: "date with someone I've never met before"
    ❑ True   ❑ False

STUDENT BOOK (PRE-INTERMEDIATE)

ON A DATE • *"He stood me up!"*

DIALOGUE USING SLANG & IDIOMS

READ THE FOLLOWING DIALOGUE. CAN YOU UNDERSTAND ALL THE WORDS AND EXPRESSIONS IN RED?

Susan is telling Melanie about her date.

Melanie: You have to tell me about your **blind date**. How was it? Was he **drop-dead gorgeous**? Was it **love at first sight**?

Susan: Hardly! First of all, I waited for an hour before he finally picked me up. I just assumed that I was being **stood up**. Then when he finally did **show up**, I opened the door to find the biggest **nerd** standing there! By the end of the evening, he told me that he had a **crush on** me and then started talking about **tying the knot**!

Melanie: On the first date?! It was probably just **puppy love**. Listen, my advice to you is that the next time he **asks you out**, just **turn him down** and run in the opposite direction! Whatever you do, you certainly don't want to **lead him on**!

Susan: I'm supposed to go out with another guy next week but for now, I've decided I have to **break our date**. I just can't go through this again.

Melanie: Now, don't **dump** him before you even meet him! He may be a great guy for you. Just make sure there are **no strings attached** before you go out.

Susan: Fine. <u>You</u> go out with him.

STREET TALK: ESSENTIAL AMERICAN SLANG & IDIOMS

DIALOGUE USING STANDARD ENGLISH

FILL IN THE BLANKS WITH THE CORRECT MEANING OF THE SLANG WORDS AND IDIOMS IN RED FROM THE OPPOSITE PAGE.

Susan is telling Melanie about her date.

Melanie: You have to tell me about your _____? How was it? Was he _____? Was it _____?

Susan: Hardly! First of all, I waited for an hour before he finally picked me up. I just assumed that I was being _____. Then when he finally did _____, I opened the door to find the biggest _____ standing there! By the end of the evening, he told me that he had a _____ me and then started talking about _____!

Melanie: On the first date?! It was probably just _____. Listen, my advice to you is that the next time he _____, just _____ and run in the opposite direction! Whatever you do, you certainly don't want to _____!

Susan: I'm supposed to go out with another guy next week but for now, I've decided I have to _____. I just can't go through this again.

Melanie: Now, don't _____ him before you even meet him! He may be a great guy for you. Just make sure there are _____ before you go out.

Susan: Fine. *You* go out with him.

STUDENT BOOK (PRE-INTERMEDIATE)   121

ON A DATE • *"He stood me up!"*

THE SAME DIALOGUE USING "REAL SPEAK"

Susan's telling Melanie aboud 'er date.

Melanie: Ya hafta tell me about cher **blin' date**? How was it? Was 'e **drop-dead gorgeous**? Was it **love 'it firs' sight**?

Susan: Hardly! First of all, I waided fer 'n hour b'fore 'e fin'lly picked me up. I just assumed th'd I w'z being **stood up**. Then when 'e fin'lly did **show up**, I open' the door da fin' the bigges' **nerd** standing there! By the end 'a the ev'ning, he told me thad 'e had a **crush on** me an' then starded talking about **tying the knot**!

Melanie: On the firs' date?! It w'z prob'ly jus' **puppy love**. Listen, my advice ta you is that the nex' time 'e **asks you out**, jus' **turn 'im down** an' run 'n the opposite direction! Whadever ya do, ya certainly don't wanna **lead 'im on**!

Susan: I'm sapposta go out with another guy next week b't fer now, I've decided I hafta **break 'ar date**. I jus' can't go through this again.

Melanie: Now, don't **dump** 'im b'fore ya even meed 'im! He may be a great guy fer you. Jus' make sher there'er **no strings attached** b'fore ya go out.

Susan: Fine. <u>You</u> go out with 'im.

A CLOSER LOOK AT "REAL SPEAK"

HAVE TO = HAFTA

RULE: Often in everyday speech, "have to" is pronounced **hafta**.

HOW DO WE GET FROM "HAVE TO" TO HAFTA?

I have to leave early today.

⬇

I ha~~ve t~~o leave early today.

In the phrase "have to," the "e" is silent and the "v" sound changes to "f."

⬇

I haf tuh leave early today.

All unstressed short vowels (such as the *o* in "*to*") are commonly pronounced *uh* (often seen in the dictionary as the symbol: ə).

⬇

I **hafta** leave early today.

This shortened version of *"have to"* is extremely common in everyday speech and is sometimes seen spelled as: **hafta**.

STUDENT BOOK (PRE-INTERMEDIATE)

STREET TALK: *ESSENTIAL AMERICAN SLANG & IDIOMS*

PRACTICE USING "REAL SPEAK"

SPEAKING

GROUP ACTIVITY

A. YOU WRITE THE SONGS...
Popular songs often use casual pronunciation. Below is the chorus to a song written in "real speak." Listen to the melody and write your own lyrics for the verses. Now try singing the song in class!

VERSE -1-

CHORUS
We hafta sing...
We hafta dance...
We hafta make this a night of romance!

We hafta laugh...
We hafta dine...
We hafta celebrate our love. Will you be mine?

VERSE -2-

CHORUS
We hafta sing...
We hafta dance...
We hafta make this a night of romance!

We hafta laugh...
We hafta dine...
We hafta celebrate our love. Will you be mine?

STUDENT BOOK (PRE-INTERMEDIATE)

ON A DATE • *"He stood me up!"*

PRACTICE THE VOCABULARY

LISTENING

B. **WHAT WOULD YOU DO IF SOMEONE SAID...?**
Listen to the situations and check the box next to the sentence that best describes what you would do in response to what you hear.

1.
- ☐ a. bend down and tie my shoe
- ☐ b. make wedding plans
- ☐ c. get some rope

2.
- ☐ a. offer an apology
- ☐ b. offer to hold them upright for an hour
- ☐ c. offer to fix their car

3.
- ☐ a. crush that person back
- ☐ b. put that person in a headlock
- ☐ c. tell the person your true feelings

4.
- ☐ a. get a broom to clean up the mess
- ☐ b. try to make plans for a later time
- ☐ c. offer to help break it

5.
- ☐ a. thank the person for the compliment
- ☐ b. run out and buy new clothing
- ☐ c. mention that the clothes were on sale

6.
- ☐ a. quickly try to revive her
- ☐ b. call an ambulance
- ☐ c. agree and explain that she's a model

7.
- ☐ a. offer to pick her back up
- ☐ b. offer to get her a bandage
- ☐ c. offer advice

8.
- ☐ a. accept and suggest going to a movie
- ☐ b. accept but insist on staying indoors
- ☐ c. accept and go stand outside

9.
- ☐ a. tell them I'll see them at 8 o'clock.
- ☐ b. tell them I'm disappointed
- ☐ c. tell them to take the elevator instead

10.
- ☐ a. suggest that chains really are stronger
- ☐ b. agree to go
- ☐ c. argue that violins are better than horns

STUDENT BOOK (PRE-INTERMEDIATE)

STREET TALK: ESSENTIAL AMERICAN SLANG & IDIOMS

SPEAKING

C. CREATE YOUR OWN STORY - *(Part 1)*
Person A goes first / Person B turns to the next page.
Take turns asking each other for words to fill in your stories. Make sure to tell each other what type of word you need as shown below each blank. When you're finished filling in the blanks, read the story together!

PAIR WORK A

THE WEEKLY Cupid Gazette

THE WEEKLY NEWSPAPER THAT SHOWS SINGLES THAT LOVE IS ALWAYS IN THE AIR

"Dear Gabby..."
by Gabby Blabber
Advice Columnist

Dear Gabby...

Today, I went out on a **blind date** with a _____ [NOUN] named _____ [FAMOUS MAN]. At first I thought I was being **stood up** because he **showed up** late. But when I took one look at his _____ [BODY PART], it was **love at first sight**! He took me to the _____ [ADJECTIVE] restaurant that serves large portions of _____ [SOMETHING TO EAT] covered in _____ [A LIQUID]. We even drank an expensive bottle of _____ [A LIQUID] with dinner. Everything was going great until a **drop-dead gorgeous** _____ [NOUN] suddenly walked into the room wearing an extremely tiny _____ [NOUN]. He just couldn't take his _____ [NOUN] off her. I'm sure he had a **crush** on her that was more than just **puppy love**. I was so mad that I **dumped** him right there and went home by _____ [NOUN]. Yesterday, he called me on the _____ [NOUN] and apologized for being such a _____ [NOUN]. In fact, he even **asked me out** again. When I **turned him down**, he kept begging me to give him one more _____ [NOUN]. What should I do?

signed... *Confused*

STUDENT BOOK (PRE-INTERMEDIATE)   125

ON A DATE • *"He stood me up!"*

SPEAKING

C. CREATE YOUR OWN STORY - *(Part 2)*
Person B starts here.

Take turns asking each other for words to fill in your stories. Make sure to tell each other what type of word you need as shown below each blank. When you're finished filling in the blanks, read the story together!

THE WEEKLY Cupid Gazette
THE WEEKLY NEWSPAPER THAT SHOWS SINGLES THAT LOVE IS ALWAYS IN THE AIR

"Dear Gabby..."
by Gabby Blabber
Advice Columnist

Dear Confused...

Before you dump the _____ (NOUN) completely, you should give him a second chance. You certainly don't want to lead him on, but you don't want to _____ (VERB) him either. If he asks you out again, and doesn't break the date or stand you up, just go out and have a really good _____ (NOUN). And if he looks at another _____ (NOUN) and starts ignoring you, then take action. In fact, if you really want to impress him, make sure to wear a nice _____ (COLOR) _____ (NOUN) on your next date. He'll think you're drop-dead gorgeous! In fact, he'll be so impressed that he won't even be able to _____ (VERB). He certainly does sound a lot more _____ (ADJECTIVE) than some of the nerds I've dated. So, try to be patient and enjoy the _____ (NOUN) you have together. You never know... he may ask you for your _____ (BODY PART) in marriage some day! And if he does ask you to tie the knot, I hope you'll invite me to the _____ (NOUN)!

STUDENT BOOK (PRE-INTERMEDIATE)

VOCABULARY - A Closer Look

ask someone out (to) *exp.* to ask someone to go on a date.

- *example:* Don't be so scared. Just **ask her out**. The worst thing she could say is no!
- *translation:* Don't be so scared. Just **ask her to go on a date with you**. The worst thing she could say is no!
- *as spoken:* Don't be so scared. Just **ask 'er out**. The wors' thing she could say is no!

YOU DO IT: *(Tell a short story or anecdote using "ask someone out")*

blind date *n.* • **1.** a date with someone you have never met in person • **2.** a person you are going on a date with that you have never seen in person.

- *example -1:* Tonight I'm going on a **blind date**. I hope he's better than the last one. He was so horrible!
- *translation:* Tonight I'm going on a **date with someone I've never met before**. I hope he's better than the last one. He was so horrible!
- *as spoken:* Tanight I'm going on a **blin' date**. I hope 'e's bedder th'n the last one. He w'z so horrible!
- *example -2:* Did you see Tina's **blind date**? He's gorgeous!
- *translation:* Did you see Tina's **date that she's never seen in person before**? He's gorgeous!
- *as spoken:* Did 'ju see **Tina's blin**' date? He's gorgeous!

NOTE: The difference between definitions **1.** and **2.** simply depends on the context.

YOU DO IT: *(Tell a short story or anecdote using "blind date")*

break a date (to) *exp.* to cancel a date.

- *example:* I'm sorry but I'm going to have to **break our date**. I need to go out of town on business.
- *translation:* I'm sorry but I'm going to have to **cancel our date**. I need to go out of town on business.
- *as spoken:* I'm sorry bud I'm gonna hafta **break 'ar date**. I need ta go oudda town on business.

YOU DO IT: *(Tell a short story or anecdote using "break a date")*

ON A DATE • "He stood me up!"

crush on someone (to have a) *exp.* to be infatuated with someone.

example: I think Betty has a **crush on** me. She keeps following me everywhere!

translation: I think Betty has an **infatuation with** me. She keeps following me everywhere!

as spoken: I think Betty has a **crush on** me. She keeps following me ev'rywhere!

YOU DO IT: (Tell a short story or anecdote using "have a crush on someone")

drop-dead gorgeous *exp.* extremely attractive.

example: Nancy's children are **drop-dead gorgeous**! It wouldn't surprise me if they became movie stars.

translation: Nancy's children are **extremely attractive**! It wouldn't surprise me if they became movie stars.

as spoken: Nancy's children 'er **drop-dead gorgeous**! It wouldn't saprise me if they b'came movie stars.

SYNONYM: **babe(to be a)** *n.*

YOU DO IT: (Tell a short story or anecdote using "drop-dead gorgeous")

dump someone (to) *v.* to end a relationship with someone.

example: My boyfriend just **dumped me** because he saw me with another man...and that man was my brother!

translation: My boyfriend just **ended our relationship** because he saw me with another man...and that man was my brother!

as spoken: My boyfrien' just **dumped me** cuz 'e saw me with another man...an' that man w'z my brother!

YOU DO IT: (Tell a short story or anecdote using "dump someone")

lead someone on (to) *exp.* to make someone falsely think that there is mutual interest.

example: You have to be honest and stop **leading him on**. Just tell him that you're not interested in him.

translation: You have to be honest and stop **making him think you like him when you don't**. Just tell him that you're not interested in him.

as spoken: Ya hafta be honest 'n stop **leading 'im on**. Jus' tell 'im that ch'r nod int'rested in 'im.

YOU DO IT: (Tell a short story or anecdote using "lead someone on")

love at first sight *exp.* immediate love upon seeing someone for the first time.

- *example:* When I met your father twenty years ago, it was **love at first sight**.
- *translation:* When I met your father twenty years ago, it was **immediate love upon seeing him**.
- *as spoken:* When I met ch'r father twen'y years ago, it w'z **love 'it firs' sight**.
- **YOU DO IT:** *(Tell a short story or anecdote using "love at first sight")*

nerd *n.* an individual who is foolish-looking, out-of-date in appearance, and unsophisticated.

- *example:* I've never met anyone who is so boring! And you should have seen the way he dresses. What a **nerd**!
- *translation:* I've never met anyone who is so boring! And you should have seen the way he dresses. What a **foolish-looking person**!
- *as spoken:* I've never med anyone who's so boring! An' you should'ev seen the way he dresses. Whad a **nerd**!
- **YOU DO IT:** *(Tell a short story or anecdote using "nerd")*

no strings attached *exp.* with no hidden expectations, no hidden motives.

- *example:* Would you like to go to the movies tonight? **No strings attached**.
- *translation:* Would you like to go to the movies tonight? **No hidden motives**.
- *as spoken:* Would 'ja like ta go da the movies tanight? **No strings attached**.
- **YOU DO IT:** *(Tell a short story or anecdote using "no strings attached")*

puppy love *exp.* immature love between very young people or children.

- *example:* I think my little son likes your little daughter. **Puppy love** is so sweet!
- *translation:* I think my little son likes your little daughter. **Immature love between very young children** is so sweet!
- *as spoken:* I think my liddle son likes yer liddle daughter. **Puppy love** is so sweet!
- **YOU DO IT:** *(Tell a short story or anecdote using "puppy love")*

ON A DATE • *"He stood me up!"*

show up (to) *exp.* to arrive.

example: You won't believe what time Karen finally **showed up**... two o'clock in the morning!

translation: You won't believe what time Karen finally **arrived**... two o'clock in the morning!

as spoken: You won't b'lieve what time Karen fin'lly **showed up**... two a'clock 'n the morning!

YOU DO IT: *(Tell a short story or anecdote using "show up")*

stand someone up (to) *exp.* to fail to arrive for a date.

example: Greg was supposed to meet me at seven o'clock for dinner, but he never arrived! This is the last time he's going to **stand me up**!

translation: Greg was supposed to meet me at seven o'clock for dinner, but he never arrived! This is the last time he's going to **fail to arrive for a date with me**!

as spoken: Greg w'z sapposta meet me 'it seven a'clock fer dinner, bud 'e never arrived! This is the las' time 'e's gonna **stan' me up**!

YOU DO IT: *(Tell a short story or anecdote using "stand someone up")*

tie the knot (to) *exp.* to get married.

example: I heard you and Nicholas **tied the knot** last month! Congratulations!

translation: I heard you and Nicholas **got married** last month! Congratulations!

as spoken: I heard 'ju 'n Nicholas **tied the knot** las' month! C'ngradjalations!

YOU DO IT: *(Tell a short story or anecdote using "tie the knot")*

turn someone down (to) *exp.* to decline someone's offer of going on a date.

example: I should never have listened to you. When I asked Sally out, she **turned me down**!

translation: I should never have listened to you. When I asked Sally out, she **declined my offer**!

as spoken: I should never 'ev listen' da you. When I asked Sally out, she **turn' me down**!

YOU DO IT: *(Tell a short story or anecdote using "turn someone down")*

STREET TALK: *ESSENTIAL AMERICAN SLANG & IDIOMS*

REVIEW

SOME OPPOSITES DO ATTRACT!

Now that you've learned almost 200 slang terms and idioms, this review exercise should be *a piece of cake* (which means "easy" in slang)!
Match the picture in COLUMN A with the picture in COLUMN B that has the opposite meaning by connecting the red dots.

STUDENT BOOK (PRE-INTERMEDIATE)

INDEX

ace a test (to), *p. 99*

act one's way out of a paper bag (to be unable to), *p. 35*

antsy (to be), *p. 113*

ask someone out (to), *p. 127*

B and B, *p. 47*

barf bag, *p. 59*

blah (to feel), *p. 113*

blast (to be a), *p. 11*

blind date, *p. 127*

blockbuster, *p. 35*

blow a test (to), *p. 99*

blowout, *p. 85*

bomb, *p. 35*

booked solid (to be), *p. 47*

boonies (in the), *p. 59*

bored out of one's mind (to be), *p. 113*

bounce back (to), *p. 115*

break a date (to), *p. 127*

bumped (to get), *p. 59*

bumper-to-bumper traffic, *p. 85*

carry-on, *p. 59*

checker, *p. 23*

chocaholic, *p. 71*

clunker, *p. 85*

cop, *p. 86*

cram (to), *p. 99*

crush on someone (to have a), *p. 128*

cut class (to), *p. 100*

cut down on something (to), *p. 71*

die for (to), *p. 23*

doggie bag, *p. 71*

drop a class (to), *p. 100*

drop-dead gorgeous, *p. 128*

dump someone (to), *p. 128*

Dutch (to go), *p. 72*

eyes that are bigger than one's stomach (to have), *p. 72*

F

fender-bender, *p. 86*

final, *p. 100*

flunk (to), *p. 100*

frequent flyer, *p. 60*

from scratch (to make something), *p. 23*

 G

get a grip (to), *p. 11*

get a load of someone/something (to), *p. 11*

get on someone's case (to), *p. 12*

get the show on the road (to), *p. 36*

grab a bite (to), *p. 72*

grab a cab (to), *p. 47*

 H

hang out (to), *p. 47*

hauled in (to get), *p. 86*

hit the town (to), *p. 48*

hop in (to), *p. 86*

hunk, *p. 12*

 J

jet lag (to have), *p. 60*

 K

killer, *p. 101*

 L

layover, *p. 60*

lead foot (to have a), *p. 87*

lead someone on (to), *p. 128*

leftovers, *p. 72*

line, *p. 36*

love at first sight, *p. 129*

 M

make one's mouth water (to), *p. 23*

make-up / make-up test, *p. 101*

mid-term, *p. 101*

 N

nerd, *p. 129*

no strings attached, *p. 129*

No way!, *p. 12*

 O

on someone (to be), *p. 73*

INDEX

 P

pass out (to), *p. 114*

pick up (to), *p. 24*

pig out (to), *p. 73*

pink (to be in the), *p. 114*

plug something (to), *p. 36*

pop quiz, *p. 101*

pot hole, *p. 87*

psych, *p. 102*

pull an all-nighter (to), *p. 102*

pull through (to), *p. 114*

punch it (to), *p. 87*

puppy love, *p. 129*

put someone on (to), *p. 12*

put up for the night (to), *p. 48*

 R

raring to go (to be), *p. 114*

red-eye, *p. 60*

ring up (to), *p. 24*

rip-off, *p. 24*

rock-bottom, *p. 25*

rug, *p. 13*

run a fever (to), *p. 115*

run a/the light (to), *p. 87*

run its course (to), *p. 115*

rush hour, *p. 88*

 S

sellout, *p. 36*

show up (to), *p. 130*

sick as a dog (to be as), *p. 115*

side of something (a), *p. 73*

sightseeing (to go), *p. 48*

skip something (to), *p. 73*

slash prices (to), *p. 25*

sleep in (to), *p. 48*

sleeper, *p. 37*

soak up some sun (to), *p. 49*

someone (to be), *p. 13*

spin (to take a), *p. 88*

stand someone up (to), *p. 130*

standby (to be on), *p. 61*

stay up till all hours of the night (to), *p. 49*

stir crazy (to go), *p. 116*

straight A's, *p. 102*

sweet tooth (to have a), *p. 74*

 T

take a dip (to), *p. 49*

take in a movie (to), *p. 49*

take it easy (to), *p. 116*

tie the knot (to), *p. 130*

total a car (to), *p. 88*

travel light (to), *p. 61*

turn someone down (to), *p. 130*

two thumbs up (to give something), *p. 37*

under the weather (to be), *p. 116*

veggies, *p. 25*

What's up with..., *p. 13*

wiped out (to be), *p. 61*

wired (to be), *p. 61*

write-up, *p. 37*